Meet the Afric

- The African grey is one of 750 identified parrot species.

- The British spelling of grey is used because British sailors were among the first to bring African greys out of the jungle and keep them as pets.

- There are two subspecies of the African grey: the Congo grey and the Timneh grey. The Congo grey is gray with a solid-black beak and a bright-red tail, measuring 12 to 14 inches in length and weighing about 1 pound. The Timneh grey is smaller and darker than the Congo with a maroon tail and a pinkish cast on a black beak. Timnehs measure 10 inches in length and weigh about 10 ounces.

- Greys are good choices for owners who cannot

tole quieter than other bird specie uaded to quiet down more quickly.

- African greys are intelligent pets. Researchers estimate that they are as intelligent as dolphins, chimps and even toddlers—they have even been known to communicate in human language.

- Greys can live more than 50 years.

- Greys need higher levels of calcium in their diets than other parrot and can be fussy eaters.

- African greys can be shy around strangers.

- The African grey has an active mind and has the tendency to get bored if not provided regular stimulation and challenges. Creating a colorful environment with a variety of toys, exercise equipment and an array of food is necessary to keep your grey happy, as is regular attention.

Consulting Editor
PAMELA LEIS HIGDON

Featuring Photographs by
ERIC ILASENKO

Howell Book House
A Pearson Education Macmillan Company
1633 Broadway
New York, NY 10019

Library of Congress Cataloging-in-Publication
Data
           The essential African grey/consulting
editor, Pamela Leis Higdon; featuring photographs by Eric Ilasenko.
                  p.   cm.
     Includes index.
     ISBN 1-58245-028-5
     1. African grey parrot.   I. Higdon, Pam.
II. Ilasenko, Eric.
     SF473.P3E87   1999   98-33423
     636.6'865—dc21   CIP

Manufactured in the United States of America
10 9 8 7 6 5 4 3 2

Series Director: Michele Matrisciani
Production Team: Carrie Allen, Clint Lahnen,
   Stephanie Mohler, Dennis Sheehan,
   Terri Sheehan
Book Design: Paul Costello

ARE YOU READY?!

☐ Have you prepared your home
   and your family for your new
   African grey?

☐ Have you gotten the proper
   supplies you'll need to care for
   your bird?

☐ Have you found a veterinarian
   that you (and your grey) are
   comfortable with?

☐ Have you thought about how
   you want your bird to behave?

☐ Have you arranged your schedule to accommodate your bird's
   needs for exercise and attention?

*No matter what stage you're at with
your African Grey—still thinking
about getting one, or he's already part
of the family—this Essential guide
will provide you with the practical
information you need to understand
and care for your avian companion.
Of course you're ready—you have this
book!*

THE ESSENTIAL

African Grey

The African Grey's Senses

SMELL

African greys seem to have a poorly developed sense of smell because smells often dissipate quickly in the air (where flying birds spend their time).

TASTE

A parrot's mouth works a little differently than a mammal's. African greys have fewer taste buds, which are located on the roof of their mouths, not on the tongue like ours.

Tiny ridges on the grey's upper beak help him hold and crack seeds more easily.

TOUCH

The African grey has a well-developed sense of touch. Parrots use their feet and their mouths to touch their surroundings, to play and to determine what is safe to perch on or chew on, and what's good to eat.

SOUND

The African grey's ears are large holes located under the feathers behind and below each eye. Greys have about the same ability to distinguish sound waves and determine the location of a sound as people do, but seem to be less sensitive to higher and lower pitches than their owners.

SIGHT

African greys, like all birds, have a well-developed sense of sight. They can see detail and discern colors. Because their eyes are located on the sides of their heads, African greys rely on monocular vision, which means they can use each eye independently of the other.

CHAPTER ONE

All About African Greys

THINGS AFRICAN GREY OWNERS NEED TO KNOW

Greys are good choices for owners who cannot tolerate consistent loud noise. However, if you have allergies, it is important to know that African greys are dusty birds. Their feather dander and dust from their powder down feathers can cause or aggravate allergies. Symptoms can include sneezing, nasal congestion and itchy, watery eyes in sensitive people.

African greys are intelligent birds. Grey parrots can use that intelligence for good activities—becoming charming, talkative pets—or they can turn it against themselves—becoming nail biters or feather pullers.

Partly because of this intelligence, African greys can be demanding pets. They require consistent attention from their owners, along with an interesting environment that includes some positive mental challenges, such as a wide variety of interesting toys and sufficient attention from their caregivers, to keep them stimulated.

Dietary Considerations

African greys need higher levels of calcium in their diets than most other parrot species. If they don't receive enough calcium from their diets their bodies will remove calcium from their bones, which can leave greys vulnerable to fractures. You can provide your grey with adequate amounts of dietary calcium by offering him calcium-rich foods. The best solution is to offer calcium-rich vegetables. Carrots, for instance, contain calcium. Other calcium-rich foods include broccoli, kale, apricots, cabbage, endive, watercress, parsnips, beans, figs, lemons, limes, oranges, eggs, tofu, almonds and hazelnuts. You can serve these foods raw, lightly steamed or as juice.

Aside from good looks, greys have brains, too! Researchers have estimated that African greys are as intelligent as dolphins, chimps and even toddlers.

Personality Traits

African greys can be shy around strangers. If you want a boisterous parrot that will show off readily and perform tricks, a grey may not be the ideal choice for you. They keep their feathers in condition by preening and with the powder down that comes from specialized feathers. Powder down feathers break into tiny particles, which the bird distributes to the rest of his feathers as he preens, or grooms, himself.

If they are not properly socialized to being handled by all family members, African greys can become one-person birds, becoming overly attached to whoever feeds them and cleans their cage and interacts with them.

African grey chicks can be clumsy. Make your young grey feel more comfortable when you hold him or carry him by allowing him to rest his beak on your chest as he perches on your hand. Some young birds feel more secure when they are held or carried in this manner. A mature grey should balance on your hand or shoulder with no problem.

Expenses of Bird Ownership

When considering the purchase of an African grey, you must factor in the following up-front expenses: the cost of the bird; the cost of his cage and accessories; the cost of bird food, including seeds, formulated diets and fresh foods; the cost of toys; and the cost of veterinary care. The last three items are ongoing costs and must be considered over the course of 40 or 50 years, which is how long African grey parrots can live. It would not be extraordinary to spend $2,000 a year on a well-cared-for grey.

WHERE WILL YOU GET YOUR GREY?

Greys can be purchased through several sources, including bird breeders, who will advertise in bird specialty magazines, the pet section of your newspaper's classified ads or on the Internet; bird shows and marts, which offer breeders and buyers an opportunity to get together and share their love of birds; and pet stores and bird specialty stores. Once you've located a source for African greys, it's time to get down to the all-important task of selecting your pet.

Look at the birds that are available for sale. Sit down and watch them for awhile. Don't rush this important step. Do some of them seem bolder than others? Consider those first, because you want a curious, active, robust pet, rather than a shy animal that hides in a corner.

If possible, let your grey choose you. Many bird stores display their livestock on T-stands or play gyms, or a breeder may bring out a clutch of babies for you to look at. If one bird waddles right up to you and wants to play, or if one comes over to check you out and just seems to want to come home with you, that's the bird you want!

As you make your selection of the right African grey for you, you may see adult birds advertised for sale at a bird store or in the newspaper. Adopting an adult grey could be a great mistake (if the bird has a number of

It is important to acclimate your bird to as many people as possible. The end result will be a better-socialized, more outgoing pet.

3

SIGNS OF A HEALTHY GREY

Here are some of the indicators of a healthy grey. Keep them in mind when selecting your pet, and reject any birds that do not meet these criteria.

- bright, clear eyes

- a clean cere (the area above the bird's beak that covers his nares or nostrils)

- an upright posture

- a full-chested appearance

- active movement around the cage

- clean legs and vent (under the tail)

- smooth, well-groomed feathers

- a good appetite

behavioral problems), or he could be the best investment you'll ever make. Try to learn as much as you can about the bird's previous owners and spend time alone with the bird before making the decision to adopt him.

BRINGING YOUR GREY HOME

Give your grey a chance to adjust to your family's routine gradually after you bring him home. Your new pet will need some time to acclimate himself to his new environment, so be patient. After you set your grey up in his cage for the first time, spend a few minutes talking quietly to your new pet, and use his name frequently while you're talking. Describe the room he is living in, or tell him about your family.

Your Grey's Routine

After a couple of days of adjustment, your grey should start to settle into his routine. You will be able to tell when your new pet has adjusted to your home because healthy greys spend about equal amounts of time during the day eating, playing, sleeping and defecating. By observation, you will soon recognize your pet's normal routine. You may also notice that your bird fluffs or shakes his feathers to greet you, or that he chirps a greeting when you uncover his cage in the morning.

Don't become alarmed the first time you see your grey asleep. Although it may seem that your bird has lost his head or a leg, he's fine. Sleeping on one foot with his head tucked under his wing (actually with his head turned about 180° and his beak tucked into the feathers on his back) is a normal sleeping position for many parrots. Be aware, too, that your bird will often perch on one leg while resting.

GREYS AND CHILDREN

African greys and children can get along well in a household if parents remind children of the following rules when they're around the parrot:

1. Approach the cage quietly. Birds don't like to be surprised. Say the bird's name softly to let him know you're in the room and mean no harm.

2. Talk softly to the bird. Don't scream or yell at him.

3. Don't shake or hit the cage.

4. Don't poke at the bird or his cage with your fingers, sticks, pencils

African greys are sensitive to sudden changes in their environment.

5

or other items. Birds will defend their homes and will bite at intruding items, including fingers.

5. If you're allowed to take the bird out of his cage, handle him gently.

You can easily learn when your African grey wants to play, rest and eat by observing his daily regimen.

A Congo African grey parrot.

6

A Timneh African grey parrot.

6. Don't take the bird outside. In unfamiliar surroundings (such as the outdoors), birds can become confused and fly away from their owners. Many are never recovered.

7. Respect the bird's need for quiet time.

Two subspecies have been identified: the Congo grey and the Timneh grey. Both species have featherless white faces and eyes that change color as the bird matures.

The Congo grey is a gray bird with a solid black beak and a bright red tail. She measures about 12 to 14 inches in length and weighs between 450 and 500 grams, or about a pound. Congos reach maturity when they are about 2 years old and can live to be 50.

The Timneh grey is a smaller, darker bird with a maroon tail, and her black beak has a pinkish cast. She measures about 10 inches in length and weighs about 300 grams (about 10 ounces). They reach maturity at about age 2 and can live 50 years.

Other than size and coloring, there's little difference between the two subspecies.

CHAPTER TWO

Homecoming

Before you bring your feathered friend home, determine where she will live in your house or apartment. Selecting your grey's cage will be one of the most important decisions you will make for your pet, and where that cage will be located in your home is equally important. Don't wait until you bring your bird home to think this through. You'll want your new pet to settle into her surroundings right away, rather than adding to her stress by relocating her several times before selecting the right spot for the cage.

CHOOSING A CAGE

When selecting a cage for your grey, make sure the bird has room to spread her wings without touching the cage sides. Her tail should not touch the cage bottom, nor should her head

A pet shop owner demonstrates features of new parrot cages.

brush the top. A cage that measures 2 feet by 2 feet by 3 feet is the minimum size for a single grey, and bigger is often better, although some breeders believe that the sometimes clumsy greys do better in a minimum-size cage.

Examine any cage you choose carefully before making your final selection. Reject any cages that have chipped, bubbled or peeling finishes and loose pieces of galvanized wire, which can be harmful to the bird if ingested. In addition, beware of cages with any sharp interior wires or wide bar spacing. (Recommended bar spacing for greys is about $1/2$ inch.) Sharp wires could poke your bird or she could become caught between bars that are slightly wider

than recommended. Also be aware that some birds may injure themselves on ornate scrollwork that decorates some cages. Finally, make sure the cage you choose has mostly horizontal bars on it so your grey will be able to climb the cage walls easier if she wants to move from one perch level to another.

Cage Door Options

Once you've checked the overall cage quality and the bar spacing, look at the cage door. Does it open easily for you, yet remain secure enough to keep your bird in her cage when you close the door? Some African greys become quite good at letting themselves out of their cages if the cage doors do not close securely. If you discover you have a feathered Houdini on your hands, a small padlock may help keep your escape artist in her place. Avoid cages with doors that slide up. Your grey could become trapped. In her panic, she could seriously injure herself.

Other things to consider: Is the door wide enough for you to get your hand in and out of the cage comfortably? Will your bird's food bowl fit through it easily? What direction does the door open? Some bird owners prefer that their pets have a play porch on a door that opens drawbridge style, while others are happy with doors that open to the side.

Other cage door options include access doors, like this one, which allow changing of bird food without opening the cage in order to prevent escape.

9

This African grey's cage has horizontal bars for fun climbing.

Cage Tray Considerations

Next, look at the cage tray. Does it slide in and out of the cage easily? Remember that you will be changing the paper in this tray at least once a day for the rest of your bird's life (which could be 50 years with good care). Is the tray an odd shape or size? Will paper need to be cut into unusual shapes to fit in it, or will paper towels, newspapers or clean sheets of used computer paper fit easily into it? The easier the tray is to remove and reline, the more likely you will be to change the lining of the tray daily, as it should be. Can the cage tray be replaced if it becomes damaged and unusable? Ask the pet store staff before making your purchase.

While we're down here, let me briefly discuss what to put in the cage tray. I recommend clean black-and-white newsprint, paper towels or clean sheets of used computer printer paper. Sand, ground corncobs or walnut shells may be sold by your pet supply store, but I don't recommend these as cage flooring materials because they tend to make owners lazy in their cage cleaning habits. These materials tend to hide feces and discarded food quite well. This can cause a bird owner to forget to change the cage tray on the principle that if it doesn't look dirty, it must not be dirty. This line of thinking can set up a thriving, robust colony of bacteria in the bottom of your bird's cage, which can lead to a sick bird if you're not careful. Newsprint and other paper products don't hide the dirt; in fact, they seem to draw attention to it, which leads conscientious bird owners to keep their pets' homes scrupulously clean.

You may see sandpaper or "gravel paper" sold in some pet stores as a cage tray liner. This product is supposed to provide a bird with an opportunity to ingest grit, which is purported to help aid her digestion by providing coarse grinding material that will help break up food in the bird's gizzard. However, many avian experts do not believe that a pet bird needs grit, and if a bird stands on sandpaper, she could become prone to foot problems caused by the rough surface of the paper. For your pet's health, please don't use these gravel-coated papers.

You may notice that some of the cages for African greys feature cage aprons, which help keep the debris your bird will create in the course of a day off your floor and somewhat under control. Cage aprons make cleaning up after your pet quicker and easier, and they also protect your carpet or flooring from discarded food and bird droppings if your bird decides to perch on the edge of her cage.

Cage Floor

Finally, check the floor of the cage you've chosen. Does it have a grille that will keep your bird out of the debris that falls to the bottom of the cage, such as feces, seed hulls, molted feathers and discarded food? To ensure your pet's long-term good health, it's best to have a grille between your curious pet and the remains of her day in the cage tray. This grille should be about 4 inches from the bottom of the cage so your bird cannot reach the debris or the paper with her beak. Also, it's easier to keep your grey in her cage while you're cleaning the cage tray if there's a grille between the cage and the tray.

WHERE TO PUT THE CAGE

Now that you've picked the perfect cage for your pet, where will you put her in your home? Your grey will be happiest where she can feel like she's part of the family, so the living room, family room or dining room may be among the best places for your bird. Avoid keeping your bird in the bathroom or kitchen, though, because sudden temperature fluctuations or fumes from cleaning products used in those rooms could harm your pet. Another spot to avoid is a busy hall or entryway, because the activity level in these spots may be too much for your pet.

If possible, set up the cage so that it is at your eye level, because it will make servicing the cage and visiting with your pet easier for you. It will also reduce the stress on your grey, because birds like to be up high for security. Also, they do not like to have people or things looming over them, so consider items such as ceiling fans, chandeliers or swag lamps. If members of your family are particularly tall, they may want to sit next to the cage or crouch down slightly to talk to the grey.

Whichever room you select, be sure to put the cage in a secure corner (with one solid wall behind the cage to ensure your grey's sense of security) and near a window. Please don't put the cage in direct sun, though, because greys can quickly overheat. Make sure your bird will be able to see the entire room. Avoid any areas near a cooling or heating vent. Interior walls are preferable, too, because exterior walls can be subject to drastic temperature changes that can stress your bird and lead to illness.

ADDITIONAL SUPPLIES

Food and Water Dishes

Greys seem to enjoy food crocks, which are open ceramic bowls that allow them to hop up on the edge of the bowl and pick and choose what they will eat during the day. Crocks are also heavy enough to prevent mischievous birds from upending their food bowls, which can leave the bird hungry and the owner with quite a mess to clean up. You may also want to consider purchasing a cage with locking bowl holders, because bowls that are locked in place (but are still easy to remove by bird owners at mealtime) are less likely to be tipped over by your grey. For really active, mischievous greys, you can buy food and water dishes that lock in place. (A healthy bird can sit on the edge of the bowl or, most likely, the area for food dishes in the

12

Some birds have odd perching habits.

cage will need deeper bowls.) When purchasing dishes for your grey, pick up several sets so that mealtime clean-ups are quick and easy.

Perches

When choosing perches for your pet's cage, try to buy two different diameters or materials so your bird's feet won't get tired of standing on the same-sized perch of the same material day after day. Think of how tired your feet would feel if you stood on a piece of wood on your sore feet all day, then imagine how it would feel to stand on that piece of wood barefoot every day for years. Sounds pretty uncomfortable, doesn't it? That's basically what your bird has to look forward to if you don't vary her perching choices.

The recommended diameter for African grey perches is 1 inch, so try to buy one perch that's this size and one that is slightly larger (1^1/$_2$ inches, for example) to give your pet a chance to stretch her foot muscles. Look for flat perches or those made of manzanita branches, which offer a variety of diameters for perching. Birds spend almost all of their lives standing, so keeping their feet healthy is important. Also, avian foot problems are

African greys need visual stimulation, so stock up on a variety of toys in an array of colors.

13

much easier to prevent than they are to treat.

You'll probably notice a lot of different kinds of perches when you visit your pet store. Along with the traditional wooden dowels, bird owners can now purchase perches made from manzanita branches, PVC tubes, tightly woven rope, terra-cotta or concrete.

Manzanita offers birds varied diameters on the same perch, along with chewing possibilities, while PVC is pretty indestructible. (Make sure any PVC perches you offer your bird have been scuffed slightly with sandpaper

GETTING STARTED

Here's what you'll need to look for at the pet store to set your grey up right.

- a cage

- food and water bowls (at least two sets of each for easier dish changing and cage cleaning)

- perches of varying diameters and materials

- a sturdy scrub brush to clean the perches

- food (a good-quality fresh seeds mixture and a formulated diet, such as pellets or crumbles)

- a variety of safe, fun toys

- a cage cover (optional; an old sheet or towel that is free of holes and ravels will serve this purpose nicely)

- a play gym to allow your grey time out of her cage and a place to exercise

to improve traction on the perch.) Rope perches also offer varied diameter and a softer perching surface than wood or plastic, and terra-cotta and concrete provide slightly abrasive surfaces that birds can use to groom their beaks without severely damaging the skin on their feet in the process. Some bird owners have reported that their pets have suffered foot abrasions with these perches, however; watch your pet carefully for signs of sore feet (an inability to perch or climb, favoring a foot or raw, sore skin on the feet) if you choose to use these perches in your pet's cage. If your bird shows signs of lameness, remove the abrasive perches immedi-ately and arrange for your avian veterinarian to examine your bird.

To further help your bird avoid foot problems, do not use sandpaper cover on her perches. These sleeves, touted as nail-trimming devices, really do little to trim a parrot's nails because birds don't usually drag their nails along their perches. What the sandpaper perch covers are good at doing, though, is abrading the surface of your grey's feet, which can leave them moving about the cage painful for your pet.

When placing perches in your bird's cage, try to vary the heights. Don't place any perches over food or water dishes, because birds can and will contaminate food or water by defecating in it. Finally, place one perch higher than the rest for a nighttime sleeping roost. Greys and other parrots like to sleep on the highest point they can find to perch, so please provide this security for your pet.

14

The Cage Cover

One important, but sometimes over-looked, accessory is the cage cover. Be sure that you have something to cover your grey's cage with when it's time to put your pet to sleep each night. The act of covering the cage may calm a pet bird and convince her that it's really time to go to bed, although she may hear the sounds of an active family evening in the background. You may also want to cover your grey's cage during the day to calm her if she becomes frightened or to quiet her if she should burst into loud vocalizations.

You can purchase a cage cover, or you can use an old sheet, blanket or towel that is clean and free of holes. Be aware that some birds like to chew on their cage covers through the cage bars. If your bird does this, replace the cover when it becomes too worn to do its job effectively. Replacing a well-chewed cover will also help keep your bird from becoming entangled in the cover or caught in a ragged clump of threads. Some birds have injured themselves quite severely by becoming caught in a worn cage cover, so help keep your pet safe from this hazard. Your bird may not want to be covered. If she

GAMES

You can also play games with your African grey to amuse her and yourself. Here are some examples:

The Shell Game A variation from the carnival sideshow. In the avian version, you can hide a favorite treat under a nut cup or paper muffin cup and let your bird guess which shell hides the prize. When she finds the treat let her eat it.

The Great Escape Offer your bird a clean, knotted-up piece of rope or vegetable-tanned leather and see how long it takes your pet to untie the knots.

The Mechanic Give your grey a clean nut and bolt with the nut screwed on and see how long it takes her to undo the nut. Make sure the nut and bolt are large enough that your pet won't swallow either accidentally.

Peek-a-Boo Put a beach towel over your bird, then let her work her way out from under it.

Tug-of-War Give your bird one end of an empty paper towel roll and tug gently. Chances are your parrot won't easily let go, or if she does, she will quickly be back for more!

In addition to playing games with you, your grey should learn how to entertain herself from an early age so she does not become overly dependent on you. Overdependence may lead to feather picking if the bird feels neglected.

15

appears frightened or if you know she's never been covered before, leave the cover off.

ENTERTAINING YOUR GREY

Your new pet has an active, agile mind that needs regular stimulation and challenges. A bored bird is often a destructive, noisy bird and doesn't make an ideal pet. Offer an array of toys and an interesting variety of food, both in the morning and in the evening; your grey may also find mealtime more enjoyable and mentally stimulating.

When no one is home, leave some background noise on for your grey, such as a radio or television, so that her environment doesn't become too quiet.

Be sure to interact and spend quality time with your African grey by cuddling with her on the couch, watching TV together or inviting her to keep you company while you work.

Choosing the Right Toys

Toys for an African grey can be as complex as you care to purchase or as simple as an empty paper towel roll. Depending on her mood, your grey can be captivated by an intricate toy with many pieces of wood strung together on knotted leather thongs, or she can be entertained by daintily nibbling on subscription cards torn out of magazines.

SIZE

First, is the toy the right size for your bird? Large toys can be intimidating to these medium-size birds, which makes the birds less likely to play with them. On the other end of the spectrum, these parrots can easily destroy toys designed for smaller birds, and

Your African grey will enjoy the challenges of her very own play gym.

they can injure themselves severely in the process.

SAFETY FIRST

Next, is the toy safe? Good choices include sturdy wooden toys (either undyed or painted with bird-safe vegetable dye or food coloring) strung on closed-link chains or vegetable tanned leather thongs, and rope toys. If you purchase rope toys for your grey, make sure her nails are trimmed regularly to prevent them from snagging in the rope. Discard a toy when it becomes frayed to prevent accidents from happening.

Unsafe items to watch out for include brittle plastic toys that can be shattered easily by a grey's beak, lead-weighted toys that can be cracked open to expose the dangerous lead to curious birds, loose link chains that can catch toenails or beaks or jingle-type bells that can trap toes, tongues or beaks.

Some entertaining toys can be made at home. Give your bird an empty paper towel roll or toilet paper tube (from unscented paper only, please), string some Cheerios on a piece of vegetable-tanned leather or offer your bird a dish of raw pasta pieces to destroy. If you plan to make wooden toys, use only

untreated lumber. Most wood available in building supply stores has been pressure treated with insecticide and/or formaldehyde.

The Play Gym

Although your grey will spend quite a bit of time in her cage, she will also need a lot of time out of her cage to exercise and to enjoy a change of scenery. A play gym can help keep your pet physically and mentally active.

If you visit a large pet store or bird specialty store, or if you look through the pages of any pet bird hobbyist magazine, you will see a variety of play gyms on display. You can choose a complicated gym with a series of ladders, swings, perches and toys, or you can purchase a simple T-stand that has a place for food and water bowls and an eye-screw or two from which you can hang toys. If you're really handy with tools, you can even construct a gym to your grey's specifications. The choice is up to you.

The best rule of thumb for buying a play gym? If it looks dangerous, don't buy it. Look for protruding metal pieces, open spaces that could catch a small body part and anything that snaps. All of these pose potential problems.

As with the cage, location of your grey's play gym will be a consideration. You will want to place the gym in a secure location in your home that is safe from other curious pets, ceiling fans, open windows and other household hazards. You will also want the gym to be in a spot frequented by your family, so your bird will have company while she plays and supervision so she doesn't get herself into trouble.

Consider placing the play gym by a window or in a spot where your bird can watch TV. She can gain additional entertainment by watching wild birds outside or whatever you're watching on TV while she's out for exercise. Think how dull your workout on the treadmill at the gym can be if you forget your tape player—your bird may need some additional visual excitement while she's working out, too!

CHAPTER THREE

Better African Grey Care

TEN STEPS TO BETTER BIRD CARE

Despite what you may think, bird keeping isn't particularly difficult. In fact, if you do only ten things for your grey for as long as you own him, your bird will have a healthy, well-adjusted life.

1. Provide a safe, secure cage in a safe location in your home. This cage should have appropriate-sized bar spacing and cage accessories that are designed for greys, and the cage should be located in a fairly active part of your home (the family room, for example) so your bird will feel as if he's part of your family and your daily routine.

2. Clean the cage regularly to protect your pet from illness and to make his surroundings more enjoyable for both of you. Would you want to live in a smelly, dirty house? Your bird doesn't like it either.

A variety of thoroughly washed fresh fruits and vegetables should be offered to your bird daily.

3. Make your home a safe environment. Close windows and doors securely before you let your bird out of his cage. Keep your bird indoors when he isn't caged and ensure that your pet doesn't chew on anything harmful (from houseplants to leaded glass lampshades to power cords). Avoid the use of any product that might cause toxic fumes, such as nonstick cookware, cleaning products, perfumes, insecticides and other aerosols.

4. Offer your grey a varied diet that includes seeds, pellets, fresh vegetables and fruits cut into small portions, and healthy people food, such as raw or cooked pasta, fresh or toasted whole-wheat bread and unsweetened breakfast cereals. Avoid feeding your pet chocolate, alcohol, avocado or highly sugared, salted or fatty foods. Provide the freshest food possible, and remove partially eaten or discarded food from the cage before it has a chance to spoil and make your pet sick. Your grey should also have access to clean, fresh drinking water at all times.

5. Establish a good working relationship with a qualified avian veterinarian early on in your bird ownership (preferably on your way home from the pet store or breeder). Don't wait for an emergency to locate a veterinarian. Take your grey to the veterinarian for regular checkups, as well as when you notice a change in his routine.

   Illnesses in birds are sometimes difficult to detect before it's too late to save the bird, so preventive care helps head off serious problems before they develop.

6. Clip your bird's wings regularly to ensure his safety.

7. Set and maintain a routine for your grey. Make sure he's fed at about the same time each day, and establish a regular playtime. Put him to bed at the same time each day.

This African grey is climbing out of his play cage, which is loaded with toys.

8. Provide an interesting environment for your bird with enough
toys to keep his active mind
occupied.

9. Leave a radio or television on for
your bird when you are away from
home, because a too-quiet environment can be stressful for many
birds, and stress can cause illness
or other problems for your pet.

10. Pay attention to your grey on a
consistent basis. Don't lavish
abundant attention on the bird
when you first bring him home,
then gradually lose interest in him.
Birds are sensitive, intelligent

creatures that will not understand
such a mixed message. Set aside
a regular portion of each day to
spend with your grey—you'll both
enjoy it and your relationship will
benefit from it.

A ROUTINE FOR YOU AND YOUR GREY

Your grey requires a certain level of
care each day to ensure his health
and well-being. Here are some of
the things you'll need to do each day
for your pet:

- Observe your pet for any changes
  in his routine. (Report any changes

to your avian veterinarian immediately.)

- Offer fresh food and remove old food. Wash food dish thoroughly with detergent and water. Rinse thoroughly and allow to dry.

- Check his seed dish and remove old seed. Refill the bowls necessary with clean, fresh seed.

Observe your pet daily to get a good sense of his normal routine.

- Provide fresh water in a clean dish and remove previous dish. Wash dish as above.

- Change the paper on the bottom of the cage.

- Let the bird out of his cage for a supervised playtime.

- Finally, you'll want to cover your bird's cage at about the same time every night to indicate bedtime. Greys seem to thrive when they have a familiar routine. When you cover the cage, you'll probably hear your bird rustling around for a while, perhaps getting a drink of water or a last mouthful of seeds

before settling in for the night. Keep in mind that your pet will require eight to ten hours of sleep a day, but you can expect that he will take naps during the day to supplement his nightly snooze.

Be Alert to Health Indicators

Your bird's droppings require daily monitoring because they can tell you a lot about his general health. Greys produce white-and-green tubular droppings. These droppings are usually composed of equal amounts of fecal material (the green portion) and urine (the white portion). A healthy grey generally eliminates about every twenty to forty minutes, although your bird may go more or less often.

Texture and consistency, along with frequency or lack of droppings, can let you know how your pet is feeling. For instance, if a bird eats a lot of fruits and vegetables, his droppings are generally looser and more watery than a bird that eats primarily seeds. But watery droppings can also indicate illness, such as diabetes or kidney problems, that cause a bird to drink more water than usual.

Color can also give an indication of health. Birds that have psittacosis (a contagious disease in birds that

Keep a close eye on toys made of rope and/or wood and replace them when frayed or chipped.

This African grey enjoys chomping on a fresh apple chunk.

Birds that overindulge on beets, for instance, produce bright red droppings that can look as though the bird has suffered some serious internal injuries. Birds that overdo sweet potatoes, blueberries or raspberries produce orange, blue or red droppings, respectively.

As part of your daily cage cleaning and observation of your feathered friend, look at his droppings carefully. Learn what is normal for your bird in terms of color, consistency and frequency, and report any changes to your avian veterinarian promptly.

usually involves the digestive tract—also known as "parrot fever") typically have bright, lime-green droppings, while healthy birds have avocado- or darker-green-and-white droppings. Birds with liver problems may produce droppings that are yellowish or reddish, while birds that have internal bleeding will produce dark, tarry droppings.

But a color change doesn't necessarily indicate poor health. For instance, birds that eat pelleted diets tend to have darker droppings than their seed-eating companions, while parrots that have splurged on a certain fresh food soon have droppings with that characteristic color.

Weekly Chores

Some of your weekly chores will include:

Removing old food from cage bars and from the corners of the cage, where it invariably falls;

Removing, scraping and replacing the perches to keep them clean and free of debris, perhaps sanding them lightly with coarse grain sandpaper to clean them further and improve perch traction for your pet;

Rotating toys in your bird's cage to keep them interesting. Remember to discard any toys that show excessive signs of wear (frayed rope, cracked plastic or well-chewed wood).

You can simplify the weekly cage cleaning process by placing the cage in the shower and letting hot water do some of the work. Be sure to remove your bird, his food and water dishes, the cage tray paper and his toys before putting the cage into the shower. You can let the hot water run over the cage for a few minutes, then scrub at any stuck-on food with an old toothbrush or some fine-grade steel wool.

Rinse the cage thoroughly and dry it completely before returning your bird and his accessories to the cage. You can air dry them in the sun if you wish.

Seasonal Needs

Warm weather requires extra vigilance on the part of a pet bird owner to ensure that the pet remains comfortable. To keep your pet cool, keep him out of direct sun, offer him lots of fresh vegetables and fruits (remove these fresh foods from the cage after no more than four hours to prevent your bird from eating spoiled food) and mist him lightly with a clean

spray bottle (filled with water only) that is used solely for birdie showers.

Warm weather may also bring out a host of insect pests to bedevil you and your bird. Depending on where you live, you may see ants, flies, mosquitoes or other bugs around your bird's cage as the temperature rises. Take care to keep your bird's cage scrupulously clean to discourage any pests, and remove any fresh foods and seed hulls frequently to keep insects out of your bird's food bowl.

Finally, in cases of severe infestation, you may have to use camicide or other bird-safe insecticides to reduce the insect population. (Remove your bird from the area of infestation

25

WARM WEATHER WARNING

On a warm day, you may notice your bird sitting with his wings held away from his body, rolling his tongue and holding his mouth open. This is how a bird cools himself off. Watch your bird carefully on warm days because he can overheat quickly and may suffer heatstroke, which requires veterinary care. If you live in a warm climate, ask your avian veterinarian how you can protect your bird from this potentially serious problem.

before spraying.) If the problem becomes severe enough to require professional exterminators, make arrangements to have your bird out of the house for at least twenty-four hours after spraying has taken place.

By the same token, pay attention to your pet's needs when the weather turns cooler. You may want to use a heavier cage cover, especially if you lower the heat in your home at bedtime, or you may want to move the bird's cage to another location in your home that is warmer and less drafty.

TRAVELING WITH YOUR AFRICAN GREY

Road Trips

To get your grey used to riding in the car, start by taking his cage (with door and cage tray well secured) out to your car and placing it inside. Make sure that your car is cool before you do this, because your grey can suffer heatstroke if you place him in a hot car and leave him there.

When your bird seems comfortable sitting in his cage in your car, take him for a short drive, such as around the block. If your bird seems to enjoy the ride (he eats, sings, whistles, talks and generally acts like nothing is wrong), then you have a willing traveler on your hands. If he seems distressed by the ride (he sits on the floor of his cage shaking, screams or vomits), then you have a bit of work ahead of you.

Distressed birds often only need to be conditioned that car travel can be fun. You can do this by talking to your bird throughout the trip. Praise him for good behavior and reassure him that everything will be

HOLIDAY PRECAUTIONS

The holidays are exciting, frenzied and, at times, stressful. They can also be hazardous to your African grey's health. Drafts from frequently opening and closing doors can have an impact on your bird's health, and the bustle of a steady stream of visitors can add to your pet's stress level.

Chewing on holiday plants, such as poinsettia, holly and mistletoe, can make your bird sick, as can chewing on tinsel or ornaments. Round jingle-type bells can sometimes trap a curious bird's toe, beak or tongue, so keep these holiday decorations out of your bird's reach. Watch your pet around strings of lights, too, as both the bulbs and the cords can prove to be great temptations to curious beaks.

For your grey's safety, it is important to place your bird in a crate when traveling to the vet's or in case of an emergency.

fine. Offer special treats and juicy fruits (grapes, apples or citrus fruit) so that your pet will eat and avoid dehydration.

As your bird becomes accustomed to car travel, gradually increase the length of the trips. When your bird is comfortable with car rides, begin to condition him for a longer trip by packing your car as you would for a longer trip.

Travel Safely

You may be tempted to have your pet ride in your car without being confined to his cage. You may have seen pictures in magazines of birds perched on car headrests or been intrigued by the concept of an avian car seat. Please resist these temptations because your bird could easily fly out of an open car window or be injured severely in the event of an accident if he is not in a secure carrier or cage while traveling in your car. Use your car's seat belts to hold the cage safely in place.

Accommodations on the Road

If you will travel to another state, you will probably need to make hotel or motel reservations along the way. As you do, ask if the hotel or motel allows pets. (The Auto Club guidebooks and other guides often provide this information, but it doesn't hurt to check the policy as you're making reservations.) Ask for non-smoking rooms, if possible, to keep you and your bird healthy, and be prepared to clean up after your grey at the hotel or motel, because this will make it easier for bird owners who come after you to keep their pets in their rooms.

Pet Sitters

Should you choose to leave your pet at home while you're away, you have several care options available to you.

If your trusted friends and relatives live far away, you can hire a professional pet sitter. (Many advertise in the yellow pages, and some offer additional services, such as picking up mail, watering your plants and leaving lights and/or radios on to make your home look occupied while you're gone.) If you're unsure about what to look for in a pet sitter, the National Association of Pet Sitters offers the following tips:

- Look for a bonded pet sitter who carries commercial liability insurance. Ask for references and

One of the most important factors to take into consideration when choosing a pet sitter is how well the sitter interacts with your bird.

28

for a written description of services and fees.

- Arrange to have the pet sitter come to your home before you leave on your trip to meet your pet and discuss what services you would like him or her to perform while you're away. During the initial interview, evaluate the sitter. Does he or she seem comfortable with your bird? Does the sitter have experience caring for birds? Does he or she own birds?

- Ask for a written contract and discuss the availability of vet care (does he or she have an existing arrangement with your veterinarian, for example) and what arrangements the sitter makes for inclement weather or personal illness.

- Discuss what the sitter's policy is for determining when a pet owner has returned home. Does he or she visit the home until the owner's return? Will he or she call to ensure you've arrived home safely and your pets are cared for, or will you have to call and notify the sitter?

If the prospect of leaving your bird with a pet sitter doesn't appeal to you, you may be able to board your bird at your avian vet's office. In the last case, of course, you'll need to determine if your vet's office offers boarding services and if you want to risk your bird's health by exposing him to other birds during boarding.

WHEN YOU MOVE

If moving is in your future, you will need to take your grey on a trip, whether it's across town, across a state line or into another country. Your first step should be to acclimate your bird to traveling in the car. Some pet birds take to this new adventure immediately, while others become so stressed out by the trip that they become carsick. Patience and persistence are usually the keys to success if your pet falls into the latter category.

As you're packing your belongings, remember to pack a cooler or ice chest for your bird. Take along an adequate supply of your bird's present food, as well as a jug or two of the water your bird is used to drinking. Your bird will be able to handle the stress of moving better if he has familiar food and water to eat and drink along the way.

SINDBAD

Feeding your bird balanced, nutritional meals and providing him with proper socialization, love and companionship can have a profound effect on him, as Sindbad's story tells us.

When Sindbad joined Julie Rach, editor of *Bird Talk* magazine, in her home, the importation of wild-caught parrots was ending. Feather-picked from her neck to her vent and brain damaged to the point of seizures, Sindbad was a skinny, frightened creature when Julie first saw her. Today, it seems impossible that this fully feathered creature, who is in control of her faculties and filled out to the point of plumpness, can be the same bird.

Sindbad and Julie began modifying each other's behavior from the start. Julie changed Sindbad's diet from primarily sunflower seeds with few fruits to a smorgasbord of fresh produce and other healthful treats and learned to respond day or night to her insistent beak tapping on the side of her cage when she'd fallen from her perch and couldn't climb back up. Julie encouraged Sindbad to play by providing her with a variety of safe and interesting toys, and Sindbad got Julie to laugh when she bulldozed the toys off her cage and onto the floor with the subtlety of a Sherman tank. Julie improved Sindbad's health with a better diet and frequent trips to the veterinarian, and in return, Sindbad improved Julie's with her amusing antics.

30

Health Check

Before you move, make a final appointment with your bird's veterinarian. Have the bird evaluated, and ask for a health certificate (this may come in handy when crossing state lines). Also ask for a copy of your grey's records that you can take with you, or arrange to have a copy sent to your new address so your bird's new avian veterinarian will know your pet's history.

If Your Move Is Abroad

If you will be taking your bird abroad, you will need to do some advance preparation to ensure that you and your grey will make the move easily. This means contacting the United States Department of Agriculture (USDA) and asking them for information on taking a pet bird out of the country. You should also contact the consulate or embassy of the country you will be moving to, to ensure that your grey will be welcome. Ask if a health certificate is required, and if your bird may be quarantined before entering the country. If he will be quarantined, will you as the owner be responsible for making quarantine arrangements? Be aware that finding answers to these questions may take several phone calls, or a combination of letters, faxes and phone calls, and patience is the key to success. Keep in mind that travel to Mexico or Canada from the United States (and vice versa) is considered international travel. If you drive across the borders and return to the United States without proper paperwork, the USDA will confiscate your bird.

Make sure your African grey receives a clean bill of health from the vet before you take him out of the country.

31

CHAPTER FOUR

Attributes of the African Grey

ATTENTION-GETTING BEHAVIORS

As your grey becomes more settled in your home, don't be surprised if you hear subtle little fluffs coming from under the cage cover first thing in the morning. It's as if your bird is saying, "I hear that you're up. I'm up, too. Don't forget to uncover me and play with me!" Other attention-getting behaviors include gently shaking toys, sneezing or soft vocalizations. A bold grey may learn to get your attention by saying "Good morning"—in a perfect imitation of your voice—or she may call your name in a voice that sounds like another member of the family.

Bat Bird

"Bat Bird" is a term used to describe a bird that enjoys hanging upside down from the curtains, drapery rods or inside her cage. Some greys are more prone to this behavior than others. It's perfectly normal, but a bit unsettling if you aren't ready for it! This is one way that greys stretch, exercise and keep busy.

Don't be surprised if your bird hangs upside down for a change of pace.

Beak Grinding

If you hear your bird making odd little grinding noises as she's drifting off to sleep, don't be alarmed! Beak grinding is a sign of a contented pet bird, and it's commonly heard as a bird settles in for the night or for an afternoon nap.

Beak Wiping

After a meal, it's common for a grey to wipe her beak against a perch, on your sleeve (if your arm happens to be handy) or on the cage floor or bars and toys to clean it.

Birdie Aerobics

In a sudden bout of stretching that all parrots seem prone to, an otherwise calm bird will suddenly grab the cage bars and stretch the wing and leg muscles on one side of her body. She may also raise both wings in imitation of an eagle. This is normal behavior.

Catnaps

Don't be surprised if you catch your grey taking a little catnap during the day. As long as you see no other indications of illness, such as a loss of appetite or a fluffed-up appearance, there is no need to worry if your pet sleeps during the day.

Feather Picking

African grey owners need to understand what feather picking is because greys seem more prone to it than many other parrot species. Don't confuse picking with normal preening. Once feather picking begins, it may

Just a little cat-nap is all this African grey needs to catch up on some beauty sleep.

Your African grey may use fluffing as a way to greet you.

be difficult to get a bird to stop. Although it looks painful to us, some birds find the routine of pulling out their feathers emotionally soothing. Greys that suddenly begin picking their feathers, especially those under the wings, may have an intestinal parasite called giardia. If you notice that your bird suddenly starts pulling her feathers out, contact your avian veterinarian for an evaluation to determine if the cause is physical or emotional.

Fluffing

This is often a prelude to preening or a tension releaser. If your bird fluffs up, stays fluffed and resembles a feathered pine cone, however, contact your avian veterinarian for an appointment because fluffed feathers can be an indicator of illness.

Growling

If your grey growls, it's because the bird is frightened of something in her environment that she's trying to scare away with the growling. Determine the cause and eliminate it if possible. Greys also growl when they are angry. If your grey growls at you or someone else, avoid a confrontation, which might result in the bird biting her antagonist.

Mutual Preening

This is part of the preening behavior described below, and it can take place between birds or between birds and their owners. It is a sign of affection reserved for best friends or mates, so consider it an honor if your grey wants to preen your eyebrows, hair, mustache or beard, or your arms and hands. If your grey wants to be preened, she will approach you with her head down and will gently nudge her head under your hand as if to tell you exactly where she wants to be scratched and petted.

Pair Bonding

Not only do mated pairs bond, but best bird buddies of the same sex will demonstrate some of the same behavior, including sitting close to each other, preening each other and mimicking the other's actions, such as stretching or scratching, often at the same time.

Possessiveness

Greys may become overly attached to one person in the household, especially if that same person is the one who is primarily responsible for their care. Indications of a possessive grey can include growling and other threatening gestures made toward other family members, and pair bonding behavior with the chosen family member.

You can keep your grey from becoming possessive by having all

FEATHERED WARNINGS

Some of the most fascinating things about your bird are her feathers. Your bird uses feathers for movement, warmth and balance, among other things. The following are some feather-related behaviors that can indicate health problems for your grey.

Fluffing: A healthy grey will fluff before preening, or for short periods. If your grey seems to remain fluffed for an extended period, see your avian veterinarian. This can be a sign of illness in birds.

Mutual Preening: Two birds will preen each other affectionately, but if you notice excessive feather loss, make sure one bird is not picking on the other and pulling out healthy feathers.

Feather Picking: A healthy bird will preen often to keep her feathers in top shape. However, a bird under stress may start to preen excessively and severe feather loss can result.

35

Parrots often bond with other species—like this African grey and blue fronted Amazon parrot.

members of the family spend time with your bird from the time you first bring her home. Encourage different members of the family to feed the bird and clean her cage, and make sure all family members play with the bird and socialize her while she's out of her cage.

Preening

Preening is part of a grey's normal routine. You will see your bird ruffling and straightening her feathers each day. She will also take oil from the uropygial or preen gland at the base of her tail and put the oil on the rest of her feathers, so don't be

concerned if you see your pet seeming to peck or bite at her tail. If, during molting, your bird seems to remove whole feathers, don't panic! Old, worn feathers are pushed out by incoming new ones, which makes the old feathers loose and easy to remove.

Regurgitating

If you see that your bird is pinning her eyes, bobbing her head and pumping her neck and crop muscles, she is about to regurgitate some food for you. Birds regurgitate to their mates during breeding season and to their young while raising chicks. It is a mark of great affection to have your bird regurgitate for you, so try not to be too disgusted if your pet starts bringing up her last meal for you.

Resting on One Foot

Do not be alarmed if you see your grey occasionally resting on only one foot. This is normal behavior (the resting foot is often drawn up into the belly feathers). If you see your bird always using both feet to perch, please contact your avian veterinarian, because this can indicate a health problem.

Screaming

Well-cared-for greys will vocalize quietly (see separate entry for vocalization), but birds that feel neglected and that have little attention paid to them may become screamers. Once a bird becomes a screamer, it can be a difficult habit to break, particularly since the bird feels rewarded with any negative attention she gets every time she screams. You may not see your attention as a reward, but from the bird's point of view, she gets to see you and to hear from you as you tell her (often in a loud, dramatic way) to be quiet.

Remember to give your bird consistent attention (at least two hours

This baby grey is removing old, loose feathers to make room for incoming new ones—a process known as preening.

37

a day); provide her with an interesting environment, complete with a variety of toys and a well-balanced diet; and leave a radio or television on when you're away to provide background noise. If you do all of these things, your bird will probably not become a screamer.

Sneezing

In pet birds, sneezes are classified as either nonproductive or productive. Nonproductive sneezes are dry and clear a bird's nares (what we think of as nostrils), and are nothing to worry about. Some birds even stick a claw into their nares to induce a sneeze from time to time. Productive sneezes, on the other hand, produce a discharge and are a cause for concern. If your bird sneezes frequently and you see a discharge from her nares or notice the area around her nares is wet, contact your avian veterinarian immediately to set up an appointment to have your bird's health checked.

Stress

This can show itself in many ways in your bird's behavior, including shaking, diarrhea, rapid breathing, wing and tail fanning, screaming, feather picking, poor sleeping habits or loss of appetite. Over a period of time, stress can harm your grey's health.

To prevent your bird from becoming stressed, try to provide her with as normal and regular a routine as possible. Parrots are, for the most part, creatures of habit, and they don't always adapt well to sudden changes in their environment or schedule. But if you do have to change something, talk to your parrot about it first. It may seem crazy, but telling your bird what you're going to do before you do it may actually help reduce her stress.

Tasting/Testing Things with the Beak

Birds use their beaks and mouths to explore their world in much the same way people use their hands. For example, don't be surprised if your

This African grey Timneh parrot inspects her owner's hand with her beak.

grey reaches out to tentatively taste or bite your hand before stepping onto it the first time. Your bird isn't biting you to be mean; she's merely investigating her world and testing the strength of a new perch using the tools she has available. This is also a good way to steady herself as she moves from one perch to another.

Vocalization

Many parrots vocalize around sunrise and sunset, which may hearken back to flock behavior in the wild when parrots call to each other to start and end their days. You may notice that your pet grey calls to you when you are out of the room. This may mean that she feels lonely or that she needs some reassurance from you. Tell her that she's fine and that she's being a good bird, and the bird should settle down and begin playing or eating. If she continues to call to you, however, you may want to check on her to ensure that everything is all right in your bird's world.

Yawning

You may notice your grey yawning from time to time or seeming to

39

Although African greys are not renowned for being the cuddliest of parrots, they may learn to enjoy being petted and held.

THE ESSENTIAL AFRICAN GREY

want to pop her ears by opening her mouth wide and closing it. Some bird experts would say your bird needs more oxygen in her environment and would recommend airing out your bird room (be sure all your window and door screens are secure before opening a window or sliding glass door to let fresh air in), while other experts would tell you your pet is merely yawning or stretching her muscles. If you see no other signs of illness, such as forceful regurgitation or vomiting, accompanying the yawning, you have no cause for concern.

PETTING YOUR GREY

Some of your African grey's favorite spots to be petted may include the nape of her neck, her head (especially if you ruffle your bird's feathers gently against the grain), her eyelids and facial areas, the tips of her wings and wing folds, her crop, under her wings and at the base of her tail. Try rubbing her beak or gently pinching it with your thumb and forefinger. Your African grey will let you know what her favorite (and not so favorite) spots are.

CHAPTER FIVE

Positively Nutritious

African grey parrots can live to be 50 years of age, but many pet birds do not live past age 5. When most pet grey parrots were wild-caught imported birds, it was unusual for them to live more than a few years. Poor diet probably played a part in the significantly shortened lives of these birds. Poor diet also causes a number of health problems, including respiratory infections, poor feather condition, flaky skin and reproductive problems.

VITAMINS AND MINERALS

According to avian veterinarian Gary Gallerstein, birds require about a dozen vitamins—A, D, E, K, B_1, B_2, niacin, B_6, B_{12}, pantothenic acid, biotin, folic acid and choline—to stay healthy, but they can only partially manufacture D_3 and niacin. A balanced diet can help provide the rest.

41

This African grey is nibbling on a healthful and nutritious berry treat.

Along with the vitamins listed above, pet birds need trace amounts of some minerals to maintain good health. These minerals are calcium, phosphorus, sodium, chlorine, potassium, magnesium, iron, zinc, copper, sulfur, iodine and manganese. These can be provided with a well-balanced diet.

Avoid adding vitamin and mineral supplements to your bird's water dish, because they can act as a growth medium for bacteria. They may also cause the water to taste different to your bird, which may discourage him from drinking.

SPROUTING

To sprout seeds, you will need to soak them overnight in lukewarm water. Drain the water and let the seeds sit in a closed cupboard or other out-of-the-way place for twenty-four hours. Rinse the sprouted seeds thoroughly before offering them to your bird. If the seeds don't sprout in two or three days, they aren't fresh, and you'll need to find another source for your bird's food. To ensure that your grey has enough seeds, frequently inspect his dish and empty it of seed hulls. Try offering grey-size portions of nutritious food to your pet. Provide your grey with fresh, clean water twice a day to maintain his health.

SEEDS AND GRAINS

Ideally, your grey's diet should contain about equal parts of seed, pellets, grain and legumes, and dark green or dark orange vegetables and fruits. You can supplement these with small amounts of well-cooked meat or eggs.

The seeds, grain and legumes portion of your bird's diet can include clean, fresh seed from your local pet supply store. Try to buy your bird seed from a store where stock turns over quickly. The dusty box on the bottom shelf of a store with little traffic isn't as nutritious for your pet as a bulk purchase of seeds from a freshly filled bin in a busy shop. When you bring the seeds home, freeze them to keep them from becoming infested with seed moths.

To ensure your bird is receiving the proper nutrients from his diet, you need to know if the seed you're serving is fresh. One way to do this is to try sprouting some of the seeds. (Sprouted seeds can also tempt a finicky eater to broaden his diet.)

Be sure, too, that your pet has an adequate supply of seeds in his dish at all times. Rather than just looking in the dish while it's in the cage, take the dish out and inspect it over the trash can so you can empty the seed hulls and refill the dish easily. Other items in the group that you can offer your pet include unsweetened breakfast cereals, whole-wheat bread, cooked beans, cooked rice and pasta.

FRUITS AND VEGETABLES

Dark green or dark orange vegetables and fruits contain vitamin A, which is an important part of a bird's diet and is missing from the seeds, grains and legumes group. This vitamin helps fight infection and keeps a bird's eyes, mouth and respiratory system healthy. Some vitamin-A–rich foods are carrots,

43

Offer your grey a variety of fresh fruits and vegetables daily.

FUN WITH FRUITS AND VEGETABLES

The key to a healthful diet is variety. Try giving some of the following fruits and vegetables to your grey. Don't be surprised if it takes numerous times for him to try a new food.

Damp broccoli florets

Apple slices

Carrots

Yams

Dried red peppers

Dandelion greens

Spinach

Cantaloupe chunks

Pear slices

Fresh chili peppers

Red bell peppers

yams, sweet potatoes, broccoli, dried red peppers and dandelion greens.

Calcium is an important part of a grey's diet. To meet this need serve whole, fresh foods including carrots, broccoli, apricots, kale, cabbage, endive, watercress, eggs, tofu, almonds, limes, lemons, oranges and figs.

You may be wondering whether or not to offer frozen or canned vegetables and fruits to your bird. Some birds will eat frozen vegetables and fruits, while others turn their beaks up at the somewhat mushy texture of these foodstuffs. The high sodium content in some canned foods may make them unhealthy for your grey. Frozen and canned foods will serve your bird's needs in an emergency, but I would offer only fresh foods on a regular basis.

PROTEIN

Along with small portions of the well-cooked meat mentioned earlier, you can also offer your bird bits of tofu, water-packed tuna, fully cooked scrambled eggs, cottage cheese, unsweetened yogurt or low-fat cheese. Don't overdo the dairy products, though, because a bird's digestive system lacks the enzyme lactase, which means it is unable to fully process dairy foods.

HEALTHFUL PEOPLE FOOD

Introduce young greys to healthful people food early so that they learn to appreciate a varied diet. Some adult birds cling tenaciously to seed-only diets, which aren't healthful for them

44

in the long term. Offer adult birds fresh foods, too, in the hope that they may try something new.

Whatever healthy fresh foods you offer your pet, be sure to remove food from the cage in no more than four hours to prevent spoilage and to help keep your bird healthy. Ideally, you should change the food in your bird's cage about every thirty minutes in warm weather. A grey should be all right with a tray of food to pick through in the morning, another to select from during the afternoon and a third fresh salad to nibble on for dinner.

While sharing healthy people food with your bird is completely acceptable, sharing something that you've already taken a bite of is not. Human saliva has bacteria in it that are perfectly normal for people but that are potentially toxic to birds, so please don't share partially eaten food with your pet. For your bird's health and your peace of mind, get him his own portion or plate.

By the same token, please don't kiss your grey on the beak (kiss him on top of his head instead) or allow your bird to put his head into your mouth, nibble on your lips or preen

Uh-oh! This African grey has gotten his claws on a hot dog— definitely not healthy for birds.

your teeth. Although you may see birds doing this on television or in pictures in a magazine and think it's a cute trick, it's really unsafe for your bird's health and well-being.

WATER

You will need to provide your grey with fresh, clean water twice a day to maintain his good health. You may want to provide your bird water in a shallow dish, or you may find that a water bottle does the trick. If you are considering a water bottle, be aware that some clever greys have been known to stuff a seed into the drinking tube, which allows all the water to drain out of the bottle. This creates a thirsty bird and a soggy cage.

FOODS TO STAY AWAY FROM

Foods considered harmful to pet birds are alcohol, rhubarb leaves, avocado (the skin and the area around the pit can be toxic), as well as highly salted, sweetened or fatty foods. You should especially avoid chocolate because it contains a chemical, theobromine, which birds cannot digest as completely as people can.

A well-balanced diet, fresh water, lots of toys and TLC will keep your bird happy and healthy.

Pelleted food is easy to serve and visually stimulating, but should not comprise a bird's entire diet.

47

Chocolate can kill your grey, so resist the temptation to share this snack with your pet. You will also want to avoid giving your bird seeds or pits from apples, apricots, cherries, peaches, pears and plums, because they can be harmful to your pet's health.

Let common sense be your guide in choosing what foods can be offered to your bird: If it's healthy for you, it's probably okay to share. However, remember to reduce the size of the portion you offer to your bird—a smaller grey-size portion will be more appealing to your pet than a larger, human-size portion.

THE PELLETED DIET OPTION

Pelleted diets are created by mixing as many as forty different nutrients into a mash and then forcing the hot mixture through a machine to form various shapes. Some pelleted diets have colors and flavors added, while others are fairly plain. These formulated diets may provide more balanced nutrition for your pet bird. Some greys accept pelleted diets quickly, while others require some persuading. We recommend against serving only pellets to your bird. No one has done adequate research on the exact nutritional needs of the African grey. This means that no pelleted diet is likely to provide all of a grey's nutritional needs. In addition, eating the same formula food each day will bore your bird. You can offer pellets with a fresh seed mix and, most important, whole fresh foods.

CHAPTER SIX

Pretty Birdie

Your grey has several grooming needs. First, she should be able to bathe regularly, and she will need to have her nails and flight feathers trimmed periodically to ensure her safety.

Although you might think that your grey's beak also needs trimming, a healthy bird supplied with enough chew toys seems to do a remarkable job of keeping her beak trimmed. If your bird's beak becomes overgrown, though, please consult your avian veterinarian. An overgrown or misshapen beak is a sign of illness. A parrot's beak contains a surprising number of blood vessels, so beak trimming is best left to the experts.

BATHING YOUR GREY

Although your grey needs to bathe, do not be surprised if she does not readily accept bathing.

You'll have to test your grey on the question of baths. Some relish them; others sneak them in by rolling in damp greens in their food bowls; while still others can hardly

Hold your bird safely in a towel when trimming her nails.

stand them. If you find that your bird likes to bathe, be sure to set bath time early enough in the day so your pet's feathers can dry before bedtime, or you can employ a blow dryer set on low to help the process along.

Your grey will not require soap as part of her bath. Under routine conditions, soap and detergent can damage a bird's feathers by removing beneficial oils, so hold the shampoo during your grey's normal clean-up routine! If your grey has gotten herself into oil, paint, wax or some other similar substance, contact your avian veterinarian.

ABOUT MITE PROTECTORS

Do not purchase mite protectors that hang on a bird's cage or conditioning products that are applied directly to a bird's feathers. Well-cared-for greys don't have mites and shouldn't be in danger of contracting them. (If your pet does have mites, veterinary care is the most effective treatment method.) Also, the fumes from some of these products are quite strong and will harm your pet's health.

Conditioners, anti-picking products and other substances that are applied to your bird's feathers will serve one purpose: to get your bird to preen herself so thoroughly that she could remove all her feathers in a particular area. If you want to encourage your bird to preen regularly and help condition her feathers, simply mist the bird regularly with clean, warm water or hold her under a gentle stream from a kitchen or bathroom faucet. Your bird will take care of the rest.

NAIL TRIMMING

Greys need their nails clipped occasionally to prevent the nails from catching on toys or perches and injuring the bird. You will need to remove only tiny portions of the nail to keep your grey's claws trimmed. Generally, a good guideline to follow is to only remove the hook on each nail, and to do this in the smallest increments possible.

You may find that you have better luck filing your bird's nails with an emery board than with conventional nail clippers. Whatever method you choose to use, stop trimming well before you reach the quick, which is difficult to see in a grey's black toenails. If you do happen to cut the nail short enough to make it bleed,

apply cornstarch or flour, followed by direct pressure, to stop the bleeding.

WING TRIMMING

The goal of a properly done wing trim is to prevent your pet from flying away or flying into a window, mirror or wall while she's out of her cage. An added benefit of trimming your pet's wings is that her inability to fly well will make her more dependent on you for transportation, which should make her more manageable. However, the bird still needs enough wing feathers so that she can glide safely to the ground if she is startled and takes flight from her cage top or play gym. Because this is a delicate balance, you may want to enlist the help of your avian veterinarian, at least the first time.

Wing trimming is a task that must be performed carefully to avoid injuring your pet, so take your time if you're doing it yourself. Please do not just take up the largest pair of kitchen shears you own and start snipping away. Owners have cut off their bird's wing tips (down to the bone) in this manner.

The first step in wing feather trimming is to assemble all the things you will need and find a quiet, well-lit place to groom your pet before you catch and trim her. Your grooming tools will include:

- a well-worn towel to wrap your bird in—one that you don't value;

- small, sharp scissors to do the actual trimming;

- needle-nosed pliers to pull any blood feathers you may cut accidentally;

- flour or cornstarch to act as styptic powder in case a blood feather is cut.

Groom your pet in a quiet, well-lit place because grooming excites some birds and causes them to become wiggly. Having good light to work under will make your job easier, and having a quiet work area may just calm your pet and make her a bit more manageable.

Once you've assembled your supplies, drape the towel over your hand and catch your bird with your toweled hand. Grab your bird by the back of her head and neck, and wrap her in the towel. Hold your bird's head securely with your thumb and index finger. (Having the bird's head covered by the towel may calm her and will give her something to chew on while you clip her wings.)

Lay the bird on her back, being careful not to constrict or compress her chest (remember, birds have no diaphragms to help them breathe), and spread her wing out carefully to look for blood feathers that are still growing in. These can be identified by their waxy, tight look and their dark red centers or quills, which are caused by the blood supply to the new feather.

If your bird has a number of blood feathers, you may want to put off trimming her wings for several days, because fully grown feathers cushion those just coming in from life's hard knocks. If your bird has

Trimming your grey's wings can help ensure that she doesn't get loose in the house, high atop curtains.

52

only one or two blood feathers, you can trim the rest accordingly.

To trim your bird's feathers, separate each one away from the other flight feathers and cut it individually (remember, the goal is to have a well-trimmed bird that's still able to glide a bit if she needs to). Use the primary coverts (the set of feathers above the primary flight feathers on your bird's wing) as a guideline as to how short you can trim.

Cut the first six to eight flight feathers starting from the tip of the wing and be sure to trim an equal number of feathers from each wing. Although some people think a bird needs only one trimmed wing, this is incorrect and could actually cause harm to a bird that tries to fly with one trimmed and one untrimmed wing by throwing her off balance.

If you cut a blood feather, remain calm. You must remove it and stop the bleeding, and panicking will do neither you nor your bird much good.

To remove a blood feather, take a pair of needle-nosed pliers and grasp the broken feather's shaft as close to the skin of your bird's wing as you can. With one steady motion, pull the feather out completely. After you've removed the feather, put a pinch of flour or cornstarch on the feather follicle (the spot you pulled the feather out of) and apply direct pressure for a few minutes until the bleeding stops. If the bleeding doesn't stop after a few minutes of direct pressure or if you can't remove the feather shaft, contact your avian veterinarian for further instructions.

Although it may seem like you're hurting your grey by removing the broken blood feather, consider this: A broken blood feather is like an open faucet. If the feather stays in, the faucet remains open and lets the blood out. Once removed, the bird's skin generally closes up behind the feather shaft and shuts off the faucet.

53

Right after a wing trim, a grey may try to fly and will find she's unsuccessful at the attempt.

Keep your bird from leaving her cage by making sure the cage door and cage tray lock securely.

54

Now that you've successfully trimmed your bird's wing feathers, congratulate yourself. You've just taken a great step toward keeping your bird safe. But don't rest on your laurels just yet; you must remember to check your bird's wing feathers and retrim them periodically (about four times a year as a minimum).

Be particularly alert after a molt, because your bird will have a whole new crop of flight feathers that needs attention. You'll be able to tell when your bird is due for a trim when she starts becoming bolder in her flying attempts. She will keep trying, and may surprise you one day with a fairly good glide across her cage or off her play gym. If this happens, get the scissors and trim those wings immediately.

Molting

At least once a year, your grey will lose her feathers. Don't be alarmed, because this is a normal process called molting. Many pet birds seem to be in a perpetual molt, with feathers falling out and coming in throughout the summer.

You can consider your bird to be in molting season when you see a lot of whole feathers in the bottom of the cage and you notice that your bird seems to have broken out in a rash of stubby little aglets (those plastic tips on the ends of your shoelaces). These are the feather sheaths that help new pinfeathers break through the skin, and they are made of keratin (the same material that makes up our fingernails). The sheaths also help protect growing feathers from damage until the feather completes its growth cycle.

You may notice that your grey is a bit more irritable during the molt; this is to be expected. Your bird may actively seek out more time with you during the molt because owners are handy to have around when a grey has an itch on the top of her head that she can't quite scratch! (Scratch these new feathers gently because some of them may still be growing in and may be sensitive to the touch.)

IF YOUR BIRD FLIES AWAY

One of the most common accidents that befalls bird owners is that a fully flighted bird escapes through an open door or window. Just because your bird has never flown before or shown any interest in leaving her cage doesn't mean that she can't fly or that she won't become disoriented once she's outside. If you don't believe it can happen, check the lost-and-found advertisements in your local newspaper for a week. Chances are many birds will turn up in the lost column, but few are ever found.

Why do lost birds never come home? Some birds fall victim to predatory animals in the wild, while others join flocks of feral, or wild, parrots (Florida and California are particularly noted for wild parrot flocks). Still other lost birds end up so far away from home because they fly wildly and frantically in any direction. And the people who find them don't advertise in the same area that the birds were lost in. Finally, some people who find lost birds don't advertise that they've been found because the finders think that whoever was unlucky or uncaring enough to lose the bird in the first place doesn't deserve to have her back.

How can you prevent your bird from becoming lost? First, make sure her wings are trimmed at regular intervals. Be sure to trim both wings evenly and remember to trim wings after your bird has molted.

Next, be sure your bird's cage door locks securely and that her cage tray cannot come loose if the cage is knocked over or dropped accidentally. Also be sure that all your window screens fit securely and are free from tears and large holes. Keep all window screens and patio doors closed when your bird is at liberty. Finally, never go outside with your bird on your shoulder.

If, despite your best efforts, your bird should escape, you must act quickly for the best chance of recovering your pet. Here are some things to keep in mind:

- If possible, keep the bird in sight. This will make chasing her easier.

- Have an audiotape of your bird's voice and a portable tape recorder available to lure your bird back home.

- Place your bird's cage in an area where your bird is likely to see it, such as on a deck or patio. Put lots of treats and food on the floor of the cage to tempt your pet back into her home.

- Use another caged bird your bird knows to attract your grey's attention.

- Alert your avian veterinarian's office that your bird has escaped. Also let the local humane society and other veterinary offices in your area know.

- Post fliers in your neighborhood describing your bird. Offer a

reward and include your phone numbers.

- Don't give up hope.

PREVENTING BIRD THEFT

Although you may want to show off your African grey and share your bird's antics with complete strangers, it may not be wise to do so. Pet birds are fairly easy to steal, and African greys can command top dollar in the pet trade because of their talking ability.

So how can a pet bird owner protect his or her parrot from being stolen? Here are a few suggestions:

- Never leave your bird unattended when she's outside.

- Consider having your bird permanently identified with a microchip. This chip, which is about the size of a large grain of rice, contains a unique number that identifies your bird. The chips can be read with special scanners that are becoming more common in humane societies and animal hospitals, and bird and owner can be reunited. You can also have a sample of your bird's DNA collected and stored as a genetic fingerprint for future identification.

- If you don't want to microchip your bird, at least take clear photographs of your pet bird. If she does tricks, make a videotape of her routine. If the bird is stolen, these photographic records can make it easier for law enforcement officials to get your bird back to you.

- Don't brag to strangers about your bird. Don't record one of your bird's clever sayings on your answering machine or allow her to ride on your shoulder when you answer the door.

- If you have many birds in your home, consider installing a home security system. Install signs in your front yard and on your windows advertising this fact.

- If you will sell birds from your home, be careful what parts of your aviary you show to prospective buyers. Be suspicious if a prospective buyer focuses too much on the price of any birds for sale.

CHAPTER SEVEN

To Good Health

P arrots are creatures of habit that sometimes react badly to changes in their surroundings, diet or daily activities. Taking the time to observe and get to know your African grey's routine is a proactive way to ensure he remains healthy. Be prepared to tell the doctor of anything new in your grey's routine and learn about your bird's anatomy, so you can easily take preventive care of your grey.

FEATHERS

Birds have several different types of feathers on their bodies. **Contour feathers** are the colorful outer feathers on a bird's body and wings. Many birds have an undercoating of down feathers that help keep them warm. **Semiplume feathers** are found on a bird's beak, nares (nostrils) and eyelids.

A bird's flight feathers can be classified into one of two types. **Primary flight feathers** are the large wing feathers that push a bird forward during flight. They are also the ones that need clipping. **Secondary flight feathers** are found on the inner wing, and they help support the bird in flight. Primary and secondary wing feathers can operate independently of each other.

To keep their feathers in good condition, healthy birds will spend a great deal of time fluffing their feathers and preening them. You may see your grey seeming to pick at the base of his tail on the top side. This is a normal behavior in which the bird removes oil from the preen gland and spreads it on his feathers. The oil also waterproofs the feathers.

Sometimes pet birds will develop white lines or small holes on the large feathers of their wings and tails. These lines or holes are referred to as stress bars or stress lines and result from the bird being under stress as the feathers were developing. If you notice stress bars on your grey's feathers, discuss them with your avian veterinarian.

You may notice some lavender feathers on your grey parrot. Don't be alarmed; it's nothing to worry about.

The bird's tail feathers assist in flight by acting as a brake and a rudder to make steering easier.

59

African grey experts believe there are a variety of causes for unusually colored feathers, ranging from excessive beta carotene in the bird's diet to old age.

Other owners of African greys may notice that their birds have red spots on their feathers or that the birds sprout red feathers where grey ones should be. Again, don't panic.

AFRICAN GREY SENSES

Sight

Birds have a well-developed sense of sight. They can see detail and they can discern colors. Be aware of this when selecting cage accessories for your pet, because some birds react to a change in the color of their food dishes. Some seem excited by a different color bowl, while others act fearful of the new item.

Because their eyes are located on the sides of their heads, most pet birds rely on monocular vision, which means that they use each eye independently of the other. If a bird really wants to study an object, you will often see him tilt his head to one side and examine the object with just one eye. Birds aren't really able to move their eyes around very much, but they compensate for this by having highly mobile necks that allow them to turn their heads about 180°.

Like cats and dogs, birds have third eyelids called nictitating membranes that you will sometimes see flick briefly across your parrot's eye. The purpose of this membrane is to keep the eyeball moist and clean. If you see your bird's nictitating membrane for more than a brief second, please contact your avian veterinarian for an evaluation. You have probably noticed that your bird lacks eyelashes.

In order to take a careful look at something, your African grey must turn his head, relying on his monocular vision.

In their place are small feathers called semiplumes that help keep dirt and dust out of the bird's eyeball.

Hearing

You may be wondering where your grey's ears are. Look carefully under the feathers behind and below each eye to find them. The ears are the somewhat-large holes in the sides of your parrot's head. Greys have about the same ability to distinguish sound waves and determine the location of the sound as people do, but birds seem to be less sensitive to higher and lower pitches than their owners.

Taste and Smell

You may be wondering how your parrot's senses of smell and taste compare to your own. Some experts believe that parrots and other pet bird species have poorly developed senses of smell and taste. Birds do have fewer taste buds in their mouths than people do. (Parrot taste buds are located in the roof of the birds' mouths, not in the tongue like ours are.)

Touch

The final sense we relate to, touch, is well developed in parrots. Parrots use

their feet and their mouths to touch their surroundings (young birds particularly seem to "mouth" everything they can get their beaks on), to play and to determine what is safe to perch on or chew on and what's good to eat.

Along with their tactile uses, a parrot's feet also have an unusual design compared to other caged birds. Look at your parrot's feet. Do you notice that two of your bird's toes point forward and two point backward? This arrangement is called zygodactyl, and it allows a parrot to hold food or toys in his foot and to climb around easily.

VISITING A VETERINARIAN

What the Veterinarian May Ask You

Bird owners should not be afraid to ask their avian veterinarians questions.

Clear nostrils and bright eyes are good indications that your bird is healthy.

Avian vets have devoted a lot of time, energy and effort to studying birds, so put this resource to use whenever you can.

What bird owners may not know is that they may be asked a number of questions by the veterinarian. When you take your bird in for an exam, be aware that the doctor may ask you for answers to these questions:

- Why is the bird here today?

- What's the bird's normal activity level like?

- How is the bird's appetite?

- What does the bird's normal diet consist of?

- Have you noticed a change in the bird's appearance lately?

Be sure to explain any changes in as much detail as you can because changes in your bird's normal behavior can indicate illness.

Common Avian Tests

After your veterinarian has completed your grey's physical examination, he or she may recommend further tests. These can include:

- Blood workups to help a doctor determine if your bird has a specific

disease and analyze how your bird's body processes enzymes, electrolytes and other chemicals.

- Radiographs or X-rays, which allow a veterinarian to study the size and shape of a bird's internal organs, along with the formation of his bones. X-rays also help doctors find foreign bodies in a bird's system.

- Microbiological exams to help a veterinarian determine if any unusual organisms (bacteria, fungi or yeast) are growing inside your bird's body.

- Fecal analysis, a study of a small sample of your bird's droppings, to determine if he has internal parasites or a bacterial or yeast infection.

After the examination, you will have a chance to talk with your veterinarian. The doctor will probably recommend a follow-up examination schedule for your pet. Most healthy birds visit the veterinarian annually, but some have to go more frequently.

SEXING GREYS

African greys are difficult to sex visually. Males look essentially like females, which can make setting up true breeding pairs impossible.

Can you tell which grey is male and which is female? If you didn't know the bird on the left was male, don't feel bad. Sexing greys is difficult to do by sight.

The following sexing methods are available: observation, DNA sexing, surgical sexing, fecal analysis and feather sexing.

Your avian veterinarian can discuss these sexing methods with you and help you decide which is the best one to use.

AVIAN ANATOMY

Skin

Your grey's skin is probably pretty difficult to see since your pet has so many feathers. If you part the feathers carefully, though, you can see your pet's thin, seemingly transparent skin and the muscles beneath it.

Modified skin cells help make up your bird's beak, cere, claws and the scales on his feet and legs.

Skeletal System

Next, let's look at your bird's skeleton. Did you know that some bird bones are hollow? They are, which makes them lighter and flying easier, but it also means that these bones may be more susceptible to breakage. For this reason, you must always handle your bird carefully! Another adaptation for flight is that the bones of a bird's wing (which correspond to our arm and hand bones) are fused for greater strength.

Birds also have air sacs in some of their bones (these are called pneumatic bones) and throughout their bodies; these air sacs help lighten the bird's body and also cool him more efficiently. Birds cannot perspire as mammals do because birds have no sweat glands, so they must have a way to cool themselves off.

Parrots have ten neck vertebrae to a human's seven. This makes a parrot's neck more free moving than a person's (a parrot can turn his head almost 180°), which can be an advantage in spotting food or predators in the wild.

During breeding season, a female bird's bones become denser as they store calcium needed to create eggshells. A female's skeleton can weigh up to 20 percent more during breeding season than it does the rest of the year because of this calcium storage.

Respiratory System

Your bird's respiratory system is a highly efficient system that works in a markedly different way from yours. Here's how your bird breathes: Air enters the system through your bird's nares, passes through his sinuses and into his throat. As it does, the air is filtered through the choana, which

is a slit that can be easily seen in the roof of many birds' mouths. The choana also helps to clean and warm the air before it goes further into the respiratory system.

After the air passes the choana, it flows through the larynx and trachea, past the syrinx or "voice box." Your bird doesn't have vocal cords like you do; rather, vibrations of the syrinx membrane are what allow our birds to make sounds.

So far it sounds similar to the way we breathe, doesn't it? Well, here's where the differences begin. As the air continues its journey past the syrinx and into the bronchi, your bird's lungs don't expand and contract to bring the air in. This is partly due to the fact that birds don't have diaphragms like people do. Instead, the bird's body wall expands and contracts, much like a fireplace bellows. This action brings air into the air sacs I mentioned earlier as part of the skeleton. This bellows action also moves air in and out of the lungs.

Although a bird's respiratory system is extremely efficient at exchanging gases in the system, two complete breaths are required to do the same work that a single breath does in humans and other mammals. This is why you may notice that your bird seems to be breathing quite quickly.

Cardiovascular System

Along with the respiratory system, your bird's cardiovascular system keeps oxygen and other nutrients moving throughout your pet's body, although the circulatory path in your grey differs from yours. In your pet bird, blood flowing from the legs, reproductive system and lower intestines passes through the kidneys on its way back to the general circulatory system.

Like you, though, your African grey has a four-chambered heart, with two atria and two ventricles. Unlike your average heart rate of 72 beats per minute, your grey's average heart rate is 340 to 600 beats per minute.

Digestive System

To keep this energy-efficient machine (your bird's body) running requires fuel (or food). This is where your bird's digestive system comes in. One of the main functions of the digestive system is to provide the fuel that maintains your bird's body temperature.

A bird's body temperature is higher than a human's. The first time a person bird-sat for friends, she worried about their cockatoo's seemingly hot feet. After another bird owner told her that birds have higher temperatures than people, she stopped worrying about the bird's warm feet.

Your African grey's digestive system begins with his beak. The size and shape of a bird's beak depend on his food-gathering needs. Compare and contrast the sharp, pointed beak of an eagle or the elongated bill of a hummingbird with the hooked beak of your parrot. Notice the underside of your bird's upper beak if you can. It has tiny ridges in it that help your grey hold and crack seeds more easily.

A parrot's mouth works a little differently than a mammal's. Parrots don't have saliva to help break down and move their food around like we do. Also, their taste buds are contained in the roofs of their mouths. Because they have few taste buds, experts think that a parrot's sense of taste is poorly developed.

After the food leaves your bird's mouth, it travels down the esophagus, where it is moistened. The food then travels to the crop, where it is moistened further and is supplied

THE ESSENTIAL AFRICAN GREY

in small increments to the bird's stomach.

After the food leaves the crop, it travels through the proventriculus, where digestive juices are added, to the gizzard, where the food is broken down into even smaller pieces. The food then travels to the small intestine, where nutrients are absorbed into the bloodstream. Anything that's leftover then travels through the large intestine to the cloaca, which is the common chamber that collects wastes before they leave the bird's body through the vent. The whole process from mouth to vent usually takes less than an hour, which is why you may notice that your bird leaves frequent, small droppings in his cage.

Along with the solid waste created by the digestive system, your grey's kidneys create urine, which is then transported through ureters to the cloaca for excretion. Unlike a mammal, a bird does not have a bladder or a urethra.

Nervous System

Your African grey's nervous system is very similar to your own. Both are made up of the brain, the spinal cord and countless nerves throughout the body that transmit messages to and from the brain.

Now that we've examined some of the similarities between avian and human anatomy, let's stop and look at some of the unusual anatomical features birds have. The first feature I'd like to discuss is probably one of the reasons you're attracted to birds: feathers. Birds are the only animals that have feathers, which serve several purposes. Feathers help birds fly, they keep birds warm, they attract the attention of potential mates and they help scare away predators.

MEDICATING YOUR GREY

Most bird owners are faced with the prospect of medicating a pet at some point. Many pet owners are unsure if they can complete the task without hurting their pets. If you have to medicate your pet, your avian veterinarian or veterinary technician should explain the process to you. In the course of the explanation, you should find out how you will administer the medication, how much of a given drug you will give your bird, how often the bird needs the medication and how long the entire course of treatment will last.

If you find that you've forgotten one or more of these steps after you arrive home with your bird and your instructions, call your vet's office for clarification to ensure that your bird receives the follow-up care from you that he needs to recover.

The most common methods of administering medications to birds are discussed completely in *The Complete Bird Owner's Handbook* by Gary A. Gallerstein, DVM. They are oral, injected and topical.

Oral Medication

This is a good route to take with birds that are small, easy to handle or underweight. The medication is usually given with a needleless plastic syringe placed in the left side of the bird's mouth and pointed toward the right side of his throat. This route is recommended to ensure that the medication gets into the bird's digestive system and not into his lungs, where aspiration pneumonia can result.

Injected Medication

Avian veterinarians consider this the most effective method of medicating birds. Some injection sites—into a vein, beneath the skin or into a bone—are used by avian veterinarians in the clinic setting. Bird

A needleless plastic syringe like this one makes it easy to give medication to your bird.

owners are usually asked to medicate their birds intramuscularly, or by injecting medication into the bird's chest muscle. This is the area of the bird's body that has the greatest muscle mass, so it is a good injection site.

You should remember to alternate the side you inject your bird on (say, left in the morning and right in the evening) to ensure that one side doesn't get overly injected and sore, and you should remain calm and talk to your bird in a soothing tone while you're administering the drugs.

Topical Medication

This method, which is far less stressful than injection, provides medication directly to part of a bird's body. Uses can include medications for eye infections, dry skin on the feet or legs or sinus problems.

GREY PARROT HEALTH CONCERNS

African grey parrots are prone to feather picking, hypocalcemia, aspergillosis, papillomas and psittacine beak and feather disease syndrome (PBFDS). Greys fed seed-only diets can also become prone to vitamin A deficiency and other nutritionally related disorders.

Hypocalcemia

Hypocalcemia (low blood calcium level) is usually indicated by occasional convulsions or tremors. Other signs of calcium deficiency can include a loss of coordination, seizures, weak bones and poor egg formation. African greys seem more prone to this problem than other parrot species.

You can supply calcium to your grey by offering him calcium-rich foods, such as low-fat cheese or yogurt, broccoli, kale, carrots, apricots, tofu, almonds, hazelnuts, endive, watercress, eggs, limes, lemons, oranges and figs or by adding a pediatric liquid calcium supplement to your bird's drinking water. In hypocalcemic birds, a high-calcium diet is usually only required until the bird's calcium levels are restored. Ask your avian veterinarian what type of diet is best for your grey.

Feeding a balanced diet is your best defense against hypocalcemia, because seed-only diets have been implicated as a cause of the condition.

Aspergillosis

Aspergillosis is caused by a fungus, aspergillus. It can settle in a bird's respiratory tract and cause breathing difficulties. This disease was once considered untreatable, but promise has been shown with some antifungal medications commonly used for humans.

Papillomas

Papillomas, which are benign tumors, can appear almost anywhere on a bird's skin, including his foot, leg, eyelid or preen gland. If a bird has a papilloma on his cloaca, the bird may appear to have a "wet raspberry" coming out of his vent. These tumors, which are caused by a virus, can appear as small, crusty lesions, or they may be raised growths that have a bumpy texture or small projections.

Many papillomas can be left untreated without harm to the bird, but some must be removed by an avian veterinarian because a bird may pick at the growth and cause it to bleed.

Psittacine Beak and Feather Disease Syndrome (PBFDS)

Psittacine beak and feather disease syndrome (PBFDS) has been a hot topic among birdkeepers for the last decade. The virus was first detected in cockatoos and was originally thought to be a cockatoo-specific

problem. It has since been determined that more than forty species of parrots, including African greys, can contract this disease, which causes a bird's feathers to become pinched or clubbed in appearance.

Other symptoms include beak fractures and mouth ulcers and a lack of powder on the feathers. This highly contagious, fatal disease is most common in birds less than 3 years of age, and there is no cure at present. A vaccine is under development. The best way to help your bird avoid PBFDS is to refrain from exposing him to other unknown birds, such as a newly purchased bird and bird marts. If you attend a bird mart, bird auction, go to a breeder's facility or handle a bird with an unknown health history, remove your clothes and take a shower *before* you handle your grey. PBFDS virus can be carried by you on your body hair if you come in contact with an infected bird.

AFRICAN GREY FIRST AID

In *The Complete Bird Owner's Handbook*, veterinarian Gary Gallerstein offers the following "don'ts" to bird owners whose birds need urgent care:

69

- Don't give a bird human medications or medications prescribed for another animal unless so directed by your veterinarian.

- Don't give your bird medications that are suggested by a friend, a store employee or a human physician.

- Don't give a bird alcohol or laxatives.

- Don't apply any oils or ointments to your bird unless your veterinarian tells you to do so.

- Don't bathe a sick bird.

Sometimes your pet will get himself into a situation that will require quick thinking and even quicker action on your part to help save your bird from serious injury or death.

The following are examples of urgent medical situations that bird owners are likely to encounter, the reason they are medical emergencies, the signs your bird might show and the recommended treatments for the problem.

Animal Bites

Infections can develop from bacteria on the biting animal's teeth and/or claws. Also, a bird's internal organs can be damaged by the bite. Sometimes the bite marks can be seen,

but often the bird shows few, if any, signs of injury.

Call your veterinarian's office and transport the bird there immediately. Treatment for shock and antibiotics are often the course of action veterinarians take to save birds that have been bitten.

Beak Injury

Infections can set in quickly if a beak is fractured or punctured.

An obvious symptom is that the bird is bleeding from his beak. This often occurs after the bird flies into a windowpane or mirror, or if he has a run-in with a rotating ceiling fan. The bird may have also cracked or damaged his beak, and portions of the beak may be missing.

Control the bleeding. Keep your bird calm and quiet. Contact your avian veterinarian's office.

Bleeding

A bird can withstand about a 20 percent loss of blood volume and still recover from an injury. In the event of external bleeding, you will see blood on the bird, his cage and his surroundings. In the case of internal bleeding, the bird may pass bloody

FIRST AID KIT

Assemble a bird owner's first aid kit so that you will have some basic supplies on hand before your bird needs them. Here's what to include:

- appropriate-size towels for catching and holding your bird
- a heating pad, heat lamp or other heat source
- a pad of paper and pencil to make notes about the bird's condition
- styptic powder, silver nitrate stick or cornstarch to stop bleeding (use styptic powder and silver nitrate stick on beak and nails only)
- blunt-tipped scissors
- nail clippers and nail file
- needle-nosed pliers to pull broken blood feathers
- blunt-end tweezers
- hydrogen peroxide or other disinfectant solution
- eye irrigation solution
- bandage materials such as gauze squares, masking tape (it doesn't stick to a bird's feathers like adhesive tape does) and gauze rolls
- Pedialyte or other energy supplement
- eye dropper
- syringes to irrigate wounds or feed sick birds
- penlight

71

A bird needs both his upper and lower beak to eat and preen properly.

droppings or bleed from his nose, mouth or vent.

For external bleeding, apply direct pressure. If the bleeding doesn't stop with direct pressure, apply a coagulant, such as styptic powder (for nails and beaks) or cornstarch or flour (for broken feathers and skin injuries). If the bleeding stops, observe the bird for the restarting of the bleeding or for shock. Call your veterinarian's office if the bird seems weak or if he

has lost a lot of blood and arrange to take the bird in for further treatment.

In the case of broken blood feathers, you may have to remove the feather shaft to stop the bleeding. To do this, grasp the feather shaft as close to the skin as you can with a pair of needle-nosed pliers and pull out the shaft with a swift, steady motion. Apply direct pressure to the skin after you remove the feather shaft. If you cannot do this, pack the bleeding feather with cornstarch or flour and call your avian veterinarian for advice.

Breathing Problems

Respiratory problems in pet birds can be life threatening. Signs are that the bird wheezes or clicks while breathing, bobs his tail, breathes with an open mouth, has discharge from his nares or swelling around his eyes. Keep the bird warm, place him in a bathroom with a hot shower running to help him breathe easier and call your veterinarian's office.

Burns

Birds that are burned severely can go into shock and may die. A burned bird has reddened skin and burnt or greasy feathers. The bird may also show signs of shock. Mist the burned area with cool water. Apply antibiotic cream or spray lightly. **Do not apply any oily or greasy substances,** including butter. If the bird seems to be in shock or the burn is widespread, contact your veterinarian's office for further instructions.

Cloacal Prolapse

This condition can present with a variety of signs: The bird's lower intestine, uterus or cloaca may protrude from the bird's vent; or the bird may have pink, red, brown or black tissue protruding from the vent.

Contact your veterinarian's office for immediate follow-up care. Your veterinarian can usually reposition the organs.

Concussion

A concussion results from a sharp blow to the head that can cause injury to the brain. Birds sometimes suffer concussions when they fly into mirrors or windows. They will seem stunned and may go into shock. Keep the bird warm, prevent him from hurting himself further and watch him carefully. Alert your veterinarian's office to the injury.

Egg Binding

The egg blocks the hen's excretory system and makes it impossible for her to eliminate waste material. Also, an egg may break inside the hen, which can lead to infection.

An egg-bound hen strains to lay eggs unsuccessfully. She becomes fluffed and lethargic, sits on the floor of her cage, may be paralyzed and may have a swollen abdomen.

SIGNS OF ILLNESS

To help your veterinarian and to keep your pet from suffering long-term health risks, keep a close eye on his daily activities and appearance. If something suddenly changes in the way your bird looks or acts, contact your veterinarian immediately. Birds naturally hide signs of illness to protect themselves from predators, so by the time a bird looks or acts sick, he may already be dangerously ill.

Some signs of illness include:

- a fluffed-up appearance
- a loss of appetite
- sleeping all the time
- a change in the appearance or number of droppings
- weight loss
- listlessness
- drooping wings
- lameness
- partially eaten food stuck to the bird's face or food regurgitated onto the cage floor
- labored breathing, with or without tail bobbing
- runny eyes or nose
- the bird stops talking or singing

If your bird shows any of these signs, please contact your avian veterinarian's office immediately.

Keep the hen warm because this sometimes helps her pass the egg. Put her and her cage into a warm bathroom with a hot shower running to increase the humidity, which may also help her pass the egg. If your bird doesn't improve shortly (within an hour), contact your avian veterinarian.

Eye Injury

Untreated eye problems may lead to blindness. Look for the following signs: swollen or pasty eyelids, discharge, cloudy eyeball, increased rubbing of the eye area. Contact your veterinarian for more information.

Fractures

A fracture is an emergency because it can cause a bird to go into shock. Depending on the type of fracture, infections can also set in.

Birds most often break bones in their legs, so be on the lookout for a bird that holds one leg at an odd angle or that never puts weight on one leg. Sudden swelling of a leg or wing or a droopy wing can also indicate fractures.

Confine the bird to his cage or a small carrier. Don't handle him unnecessarily. Keep him warm and contact your veterinarian.

Frostbite

A bird could lose toes or feet to frostbite. He could also go into shock and die as a result. The frostbitten area is very cold and dry to the touch and is pale in color.

Warm up the damaged tissue gradually in a circulating water bath. Keep your bird warm and contact your veterinarian's office for further instructions.

Inhaled or Ingested Foreign Object

Birds can develop serious respiratory or digestive problems from eating or breathing foreign objects. In the case of inhaled items, wheezing and other respiratory problems may result. In the case of consumed objects, consider whether the bird was seen playing with a small item that suddenly cannot be found.

If you suspect that your bird has inhaled or eaten something he shouldn't, contact your veterinarian's office immediately.

Lead Poisoning

Birds can die from lead poisoning. A bird with lead poisoning may act depressed or weak. He may lose his sight, or he may walk in circles at the bottom of his cage. He may regurgitate or pass droppings that resemble tomato juice.

Contact your avian veterinarian immediately. Lead poisoning requires a quick start to treatment, and the treatment may require several days or weeks to complete successfully.

Note: Lead poisoning is easily prevented by keeping birds away from common sources of lead in the home. These include stained glass items, leaded paint found in some older homes, fishing weights, drapery weights and parrot toys (some are weighted with lead) as well as costume jewelry. One item that won't cause lead poisoning is "lead" pencils. They're actually graphite.

If your grey shows signs of eye problems, contact your avian veterinarian immediately.

75

Overheating

High body temperatures can kill a bird. An overheated bird will pull his feathers close to his body. He will hold his wings away from his body, open his mouth to pant and roll his tongue in an attempt to cool himself. Birds don't have sweat glands, so they must try to cool their bodies by exposing as much of their skin's surface as they can to moving air.

Cool the bird off by putting him in front of a fan (make sure the blades are screened so the bird doesn't injure himself further), by spraying him with cool water or by having him stand in a bowl of cool water. Let the bird drink cool water if he can (if he can't, offer him cool water with an eyedropper) and contact your veterinarian.

Poisoning

Poisons can kill a bird quickly. Poisoned birds may suddenly regurgitate, have diarrhea or bloody droppings and have redness or burns around their mouths. They may also go into convulsions, become paralyzed or go into shock.

Put the poison out of your bird's reach. Contact your veterinarian for further instructions. Be prepared to take the poison with you to the vet's office in case he or she needs to contact a poison control center for further information.

Seizures

Seizures can indicate a number of serious conditions, including lead poisoning, infection, a nutritional deficiency, heatstroke and epilepsy.

The bird goes into a seizure that lasts from a few seconds to a minute. Afterward, he seems dazed and may stay on the cage floor for several hours. He may also appear unsteady and won't perch.

Keep the bird from hurting himself further by removing everything you can from his cage. Cover the bird's cage with a towel and darken the room to reduce the bird's stress level. Contact your veterinarian's office for further instructions immediately.

Shock

Shock indicates that the bird's circulatory system cannot move the blood supply around the bird's body. This is a serious condition that can lead to death if left untreated. Birds that are in shock may act depressed, they may breathe rapidly and they may have a fluffed appearance. If your bird displays these signs in conjunction with a recent accident, suspect shock and take appropriate action.

Keep your bird warm, cover his cage and transport him to your veterinarian's office as soon as possible.

HOUSEHOLD HAZARDS

Look at your home from your grey's point of view. As a responsible bird owner, you want to provide your pet with the best care possible, and part of that care requires that you essentially bird-proof your home. Let's take a room-by-room look at some of the potentially dangerous situations you should be aware of.

Bathroom

Your bird could fall into an uncovered toilet bowl and drown; he could hurt himself chewing on the cord of your blow dryer; or he could be overcome by fumes from perfume, hair spray or cleaning products, such as bleach, air freshener or toilet bowl cleaner. The bird could also become ill if he

nibbles on prescription or over-the-counter drugs in the medicine chest or he could injure himself by flying into a mirror.

Kitchen

An unsupervised bird could fly or fall into the trash can, or he could climb into the oven, dishwasher, freezer or refrigerator and be forgotten. Your bird could also land on a hot stove element, or he could fall into an uncovered pot of boiling liquid or a sizzling frying pan on the stove. The bird could also become poisoned by eating foods that are unsafe for him, such as chocolate, avocado or rhubarb leaves.

What seems like home sweet home to you can be an unsafe home for your bird.

EMERGENCY TIPS

When facing emergency situations, keep the following tips in mind:

Keep the bird warm. You can do this by putting the bird in an empty aquarium with a heating pad under him, by putting a heat lamp near the bird's cage or by putting a heating pad set on low under the bird's cage in place of the cage tray. Whatever heat sources you choose to use, make sure to keep a close eye on your bird so that he doesn't accidentally burn himself on the pad or lamp or that he doesn't chew on a power cord.

Put the bird in a dark, quiet room. This helps reduce the bird's stress.

Put the bird's food in locations that are easy to reach. Sick birds need to eat, but they may not be able to reach food in the normal locations in the cage. Sometimes, birds require hand-feeding to keep their calorie consumption steady.

Protect the bird from additional injury. If the convalescing bird is in a clear-sided aquarium, for example, you may want to put a towel over the glass to keep the bird from flying into it.

Living Room

Your pet could be injured or killed if he decided to play hide-and-seek under pillows or cushions and was accidentally sat on. Your grey could become poisoned by nibbling on a leaded-glass lampshade, or he could fly out an open window or patio door. By the same token, he could fly into a closed window or door and injure himself severely. He could become entangled in a drapery cord or a venetian blind pull or he could ingest poison by nibbling on ashes or used cigarette butts in an ashtray. In addition, he might investigate the inviting space under a recliner, only to be crushed when someone sits in the chair and leans back to recline.

Home Office

You'll have to be on your toes to keep your pet from harming himself by nibbling on potentially poisonous markers, glue sticks or crayons, or injuring himself on push pins, pens or scissors.

Other Areas of Concern

Grey owners need to know that earrings and other jewelry prove to be great temptations to these birds. Pay attention if your bird suddenly takes an interest in your jewelry (chances are a sharp tug on your earring will warn you that this is happening) because your grey's inquisitive beak

could destroy the jewelry, and the bird could swallow part of it and become ill. This is a good reason not to let your bird on your shoulder, but instead carry him so his head is at the level of your shirt pockets.

You should not keep your bird locked up in his cage all the time. On the contrary, all parrots need time out of their cages to maintain physical and mental health.

Unfortunately, potential dangers to a pet bird don't stop with the furniture and accessories. A variety of fumes can overpower your grey, such as those from cigarettes, air fresheners, insecticides, bleach, shoe polish, oven cleaners, kerosene, lighter fluid, glues, active self-cleaning ovens, hair spray, overheated non-stick cookware, paint thinner, bathroom cleaners or nail polish remover.

If you're considering a remodeling or home improvement project, think about your grey first. Fumes

This inquisitive grey is tempted to play with his owner's earrings and eyeglasses.

"SAFE" PLANTS

You're probably wondering which plants, if any, are considered safe to keep around pet birds. Here are some bird-safe plants:

- African violets

- aloe

- burro's tail

- Christmas cactus

- coleus

- edible fig (Ficus)

- fern (asparagus, Boston, bird's nest, maidenhair, ribbon, staghorn, squirrel's foot)

- gardenia

- grape ivy

- hen and chicks

- hibiscus

- jade plant

- kalanchoe

- palms (butterfly, cane, golden feather, Madagascar, European fan, sentry and pygmy date)

- pepperomia

- rubber plant

- spider plant

- yucca

from paint or formaldehyde, which can be found in carpet backing, paneling and particle board, can cause pets and people to become ill. If you are having work done on your home, consider boarding your grey at your avian veterinarian's office or at the home of a bird-loving friend or relative until the project is complete and the house is aired out fully.

Having your home fumigated for termites poses another potentially hazardous situation to your pet grey. Ask your exterminator for information about the types of chemicals that will be used in your home, and inquire if pet-safe formulas, such as electrical currents or liquid nitrogen, are available. If your house must be treated chemically, arrange to board your bird at your avian veterinarian's office or with a friend before, during and after the fumigation. Make sure your house is aired out completely before bringing your bird home, too.

If you have other pets in the home that require flea treatments, consider pyrethrin-based products. These natural flea killers are derived from chrysanthemums and, although they aren't as long-lasting as synthetic substitutes, they do knock down fleas quickly and are safer in the long run for your pets and you.

Other pets can harm your grey's health, too. A curious cat could claw or bite your pet, a dog could step on him accidentally or bite him, or another bird could break his leg or rip off his upper mandible with his beak.

PLANTS TO LOOK OUT FOR

Even common houseplants can pose a threat to your pet's health. As a general rule of thumb, if it's toxic for children, it's dangerous to your bird's health, too. Here are some plants that are considered poisonous to parrots:

- amaryllis
- bird of paradise
- calla lily
- daffodil
- dieffenbachia
- English ivy
- foxglove
- holly
- juniper
- lily-of-the-valley
- mistletoe
- oleander
- philodendron
- rhododendron
- rhubarb leaves
- sweet pea
- wisteria

This list is by no means complete. Many flowers included in arrangements are toxic if eaten, for instance.

CHAPTER EIGHT

A Matter of Fact

BIRD KEEPING THROUGH THE AGES

The ancient Egyptians are credited with being the first to keep birds, most notably pigeons. From Egypt, bird keeping spread to Greece and Rome. Some historians credit Alexander the Great with discovering the Alexandrian parakeet, and the Greeks receive credit for popularizing parrot keeping outside the birds' native lands of Africa and Asia.

Wealthy Romans built elaborate garden aviaries, and they also used mockingbirds in the entryways of their homes as feathered doorbells to announce visitors. The Romans are thought to be the first bird dealers, bringing different types of birds to Great Britain and the European continent.

Although bird keeping was still largely an upper-class fancy, the Renaissance opened it up as a hobby for the masses. Portuguese sailors introduced Europe to canaries at this time, and in the 1600s the Dutch began producing varieties of canaries for show. These birds were exported to Britain, where bird keeping became quite popular.

Around this time, in the British penal colony of Australia, a forger named Thomas Watling first described the budgerigar's ability to mimic human speech. This bird greeted Watling's employer by saying, "How do you do, Dr. White?"

In the 18th century, Duc de Nivernais, from France, wrote about his Finch aviary, a unique way to house birds in that day and age. Most birds had previously been kept in tiny cages or chained to perches. His aviary comprised a large, fine net that covered a small wooded area near his home.

As transportation became more efficient, wild birds were captured for keeping in distant parts of the world. It became possible to buy a bird whose natural habitat was continents away.

Bird keeping as we know it today can be traced to its beginning in Victorian Great Britain, when bird sellers in the British Isles would offer goldfinches and larks to ship captains

en route to the West Indies. These common European birds would then be traded in the islands for species found there.

In the United States, bird keeping was quite popular in the '50s and early '60s. It was fairly easy to find most South American birds, as well as some African greys. Budgerigars and Cockatiels from Australia were imported in large numbers, as well as some Finches and Cockatoos.

THE AFRICAN GREY'S BACKGROUND

As the name implies, the African grey parrot is a gray bird that comes from Africa. Attractive gray birds with red tails were seen around 1402 in the Canary Islands. They had been imported from West Africa. To this day, African greys are found in western and central Africa, from Guinea to northern Angola. The British spelling of grey is used in connection with these birds because British sailors and explorers were among the first to bring African greys out of their native habitat and make pets of them.

Greys were first bred outside of Africa in 1770 when a pair was coupled in France for breeding purposes. A British pair of pet birds followed

Attractive gray birds with red tails were seen around 1402 in the Canary Islands.

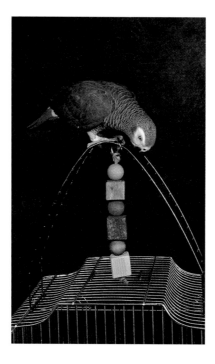

suit in the United Kingdom in 1843. This pair of birds successfully raised a single chick after the breeder fashioned a flannel nest for the hen.

Greys in America

Until about 20 years ago, most of the pet greys in the United States were imported from Africa. The situation began changing in the 1980s, when stricter importation regulations began to be enacted. By the early 1990s, almost no African greys were being brought into the United States from abroad, thanks to a combination of international laws and a reluctance on the part of airlines that once carried

Scientists are fascinated with the African grey's ability to learn. This Congo African grey parrot is learning "up" and "down" commands on a T-stand.

large shipments of birds to become involved in the now-complicated import process.

THE AMAZING ALEX

In 1977, Irene Pepperberg, PhD, purchased an African grey parrot in a Chicago pet store as part of a research project to examine animal intelligence and communication skills.

That bird is Alex, and he has proved to be an exceptional research subject. Dr. Pepperberg has learned that Alex not only uses human language to communicate, but he uses language appropriately, noting differences and similarities in objects that are shown to him. He also tells researchers the colors and materials these objects are made from.

Alex was joined in the lab by two African grey chicks in 1992. These birds began by identifying objects, such as paper or cork. They followed this by learning the concept of category, including the number of a particular item, its relative size, the material it is made from and its color. Finally, the birds learned phonemes (distinctive sounds) and how to combine them.

Alex and the other birds in Dr. Pepperberg's lab are not the first

African greys studied in this manner. Researchers in Europe developed a method of communicating with African greys in the 1940s and 1950s, and a German researcher popularized the use of the model/rival technique to teach and study African grey parrots. In this method, the teacher shows one of two students (either avian or human) an object and asks what it is. If the student identifies it correctly, the teacher gives the object to the student to examine and play with. If the student gives an incorrect answer, the teacher and the other student "model" the correct response, then the teacher asks the first student the question again. Tests conducted on Alex indicate that he can answer 80 percent of the questions asked him correctly.

Alex knows the names of almost 100 items; he can count to six; he can name about seven colors and about seven different types of materials. He has also made up his own names for some items, such as "banana cracker" to describe a banana chip, "cork nut" to ask for an almond in its shell and "rock corn" to distinguish dried corn from fresh.

PARROT TRAITS

The African grey is a type of parrot, just like the hyacinth macaw or mealy amazon. The traits that all parrot species have in common are:

- four toes—two pointing backward and two pointing forward

- curved upper beak overhanging the lower

- broad head and short neck

However, a healthy African grey measures about 11 inches to $13^{1}/_{2}$ inches from head to tip of the tail, while a full-grown scarlet macaw can easily reach 40 inches in length. African greys are a type of parrot and share similar traits, such as a broad head and short neck. African greys have shown the ability to use human language to communicate.

CHAPTER NINE

Resources

For more information on bird care, look for these books at your local library, bookstore or pet store:

BOOKS

About Parrot Care

Alderton, David, with illustrations by Graeme Stevenson. *Atlas of Parrots of the World*. Neptune, N.J.: TFH Publications Inc., 1991.

Barber, T.X. *The Human Nature of Birds*. New York: St. Martin's Press, 1993.

Bedford, Duke of. *Parrots and Parrotlike Birds*. Neptune, N.J.: TFH Publications, 1969.

Doane, Bonnie Munro and Thomas Qualkenbush. *Birdkeeper's Guide to Parrots and Macaws*. Tetra Press, 1989.

———. *Keeping African Grey Parrots*. Neptune, N.J.: TFH Publications Inc., 1995.

———. *My Parrot My Friend: An Owner's Guide to Parrot Behavior*. New York: Howell Book House, 1994.

Doane, Bonnie Munro. *The Parrot in Health and Illness: An Owner's Guide*. New York: Howell Book House, 1991.

———. *The Pleasure of Their Company: An Owner's Guide to Parrot Training*. New York: Howell Book House, 1998.

Gallerstein, Gary A. DVM. *The Complete Bird Owner's Handbook*. New York: Howell Book House, 1994.

Rach, Julie. *Why Does My Bird Do That? A Guide to Parrot Behavior*. New York: Howell Book House, 1998.

Walker, Annette, Rita Kimber and Robert Kimber. *African Grey Parrots*. New York: Barrons, 1987.

MAGAZINES

BIRD TALK
Monthly magazine devoted to pet bird ownership. Subscription information: P.O. Box 57347, Boulder, CO 80322.

BIRD TIMES
This magazine for pet bird owners is published seven times a year. Subscription information: 7-L Dundas Circle, Greensboro, NC 27407.

BIRDS USA
Annual magazine aimed at first-time bird owners. Subscription information: P.O. Box 57347, Boulder, CO 80322.

CAGED BIRD HOBBYIST
This magazine for pet-bird owners is published seven times a year. Subscription information: 5400 NW 84th Ave., Miami, FL 33166-3333.

NATURAL PET
Monthy magazine devoted to the best in natural care for all pets. Available at your local pet or bookstore.

ON-LINE RESOURCES

Bird Breeder
On-line magazine dedicated to the concerns of bird breeders who raise and sell pet birds, which can be reached at **www. birdbreeder.com.**

Bird Talk
Read *Bird Talk* magazine on-line at **www. petchannel.com/birds/default.asp.**

Other Bird-Specific Sites

www.animalnetwork.com/birds/default/ asp

www.parrottalk.com/avian.html

www. nasw.org

www.altvetmed

BIRD CLUBS

THE AFRICAN PARROT SOCIETY
P.O. Box 204
Clarinda, IA 51632-2731
www.wingscc.com/aps

THE AMERICAN FEDERATION OF AVICULTURE
P.O. Box 56218
Phoenix, AZ 85017-6218
(602) 484-0931
www2.upatsix.com/afa

AVICULTURAL SOCIETY OF AMERICA
P.O. Box 5516
Riverside, CA 92517-5517
(909) 780-4102
www2.upatsix.com/associations/asa/ member.html

INTERNATIONAL
AVICULTURAL SOCIETY
P.O. Box 280383
Memphis, TN 38168

NATIONAL CAGE BIRD
SHOW CLUB, INC.
25 Janss Rd.
Thousand Oaks, CA 91360

NATIONAL PARROT
ASSOCIATION
8 N. Hoffman Lane
Hauppage, NY 11788

NORTH AMERICAN
PARROT SOCIETY
5726 Joyce Avenue
Fort Wayne, IN 46818
www.upatsix.com/associations/naps

SOCIETY OF PARROT
BREEDERS AND
EXHIBITORS
P.O. Box 369
Groton, MA 01450
(978) 672-4568
www2.upatsix.com/spbe

INDEX

90

YOUR ESSENTIAL *African Grey* INFORMATION SHEET

Tear me out!

Put a picture of your bird
in this box

Your Bird's Name ____________________

Identifying Features ____________________

____

Date of Birth ____________________

Your Bird's Veterinarian ____________________

Address ____________________

Phone Number ____________________

Medications ____________________

Vet Emergency Number ____________________

Additional Emergency Numbers ____________________

Favorite Foods ____________________

____

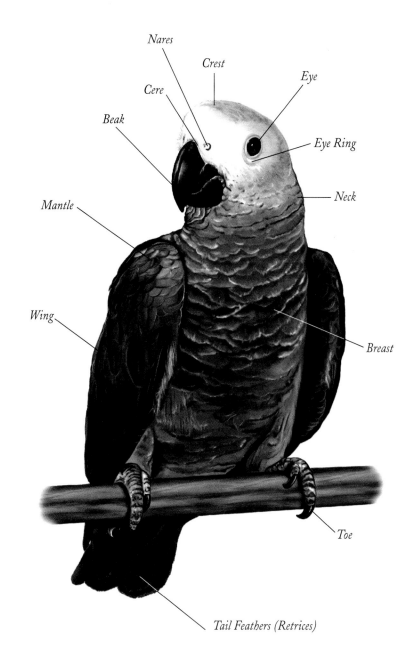

Nares

Crest

Cere

Eye

Beak

Eye Ring

Mantle

Neck

Wing

Breast

Toe

Tail Feathers (Retrices)